Praise

'Sandeep is an authority on providing best-in-class Invisalign treatment and using it as a key offering to align your team, improve the service to patients and fuel practice growth. In this book, he shares valuable insights, experience and lessons that you can apply in your dental practice or group. His connection between the team, the patient, marketing, leadership and running the practice as a business is a powerful one. Learning how he thinks, plans, and then puts those plans into action is fascinating. If you're a practice owner or leader in dentistry, you will learn a lot from reading this book.'
— **Justin Leigh**, Managing Director, Focus4Growth

'There is a great clarity of approach which gives the reader reassurance that they could follow in Sandeep's footsteps and build an equally inspiring Invisalign practice. The various models Sandeep has used throughout the book are really useful and he shows how to apply them easily and effectively. If you're a dentist about to embark on your Invisalign journey, this is the book to read.'
— **Jag Shoker**, mind coach, author and speaker

'A great book full of useful and practical suggestions for growing Invisalign within your practice.'
— **Jamie Morley**, leadership coach

MASTERING

YOUR

INVISALIGN

BUSINESS

R^ethink

First published in Great Britain in 2022
by Rethink Press (www.rethinkpress.com)

© Copyright Sandeep Kumar

To my mum and dad in India, for believing in me

To my wife Rita, for supporting and encouraging me

To Rahil and Sana, my lovely children

Contents

Foreword

I first met Dr Sandeep Kumar in early 2011, in the upstairs office at his New Street dental practice. I was then commercial leader for Align Technology's European business, and Sandeep's practice had come to my attention for being one of the largest Invisalign providers in the UK and across Europe.

At that time, patients who wanted to gain access to Invisalign clear aligners in the UK, unlike in many other European countries, were more likely to receive treatment from a general dentist than an orthodontist. Sandeep had been an early adopter of the technology and was considered one of the leading providers of this treatment option, which was still relatively unknown.

As we sat together for the first time, Sandeep explained how he thought he had the potential to do more treatments than he was currently doing. I immediately warmed to Sandeep, and not just because of his desire to grow his practice. By all conventional standards at that point, he was already performing well at around 100 treatments per year, so there was no financial incentive for him to do more with us. He would receive no additional discount, no added benefits, but there was just something about Sandeep – something you feel when you are in the presence of a person you know will succeed at whatever they turn their hand to.

Sandeep and I agreed to stay in touch and that together we would explore the possibilities of doing something different, but it wasn't until 2013 that what would become MiSmile started to take shape. At Align, we'd seen success in multiple markets by the creation of groups or networks in which like-minded individuals were coming together under a single banner, with a common purpose of growing their practices and providing a high standard of care. As we considered this model more, there was only one person I wanted to talk to: Sandeep. I knew he would see the potential in the network concept and be prepared to get involved.

I wasn't wrong: he jumped at the opportunity, investing his time and money in the concept, going 'all in'. Unfortunately, the model we created didn't work out, but Sandeep saw the potential. He agreed that there remained an opportunity, so he made a bold move and decided that he would create his own network. He would take what he'd learned and establish a group that he could lead: one where he could provide the direction, support and mentorship required to help others to build a profitable Invisalign practice.

MiSmile was born.

To have an idea is one thing; to execute it is another entirely. He'd seen a publicly traded billion-dollar company try its hand at building a network and fail, yet wasn't deterred. This is where Sandeep excels, not just because of his own hands-on and action-orientated approach, but because of the way he involves other people. He surrounded himself with people who had the experience and skillset to support him. He was generous with his time and money, forgoing profit for the sake of ensuring that the right people felt part of what he was wanting to do.

While there are many reasons that Sandeep has been successful, I believe it is his mindset and his willing-ness to acknowledge those areas where others have more experience and bring those people into his thinking in a generous and abundant way that make the biggest difference. This is why professionals across so many different areas of business and life who have worked with Sandeep would drop what they are doing to make time to support him.

The man who arrived in the UK from the humblest of beginnings has created a genuinely world-class organisation and continues to strive to improve on his already successful business by being open, inclusive and driven. I'm delighted that Sandeep has written this book and humbled that he asked me to write the foreword. The timing is perfect, as the opportunities for Invisalign providers to offer exceptional care and build a successful practice have never been greater. Sandeep is well positioned as a leader within the industry and, as is his way, he is willing to share his ideas and experience with others to inspire them to create a better way.

That's Sandeep. That's his way – MIWAY.

Wishing you much success on your journey.

Michael Smith, chief commercial officer at Sonendo

Introduction

Some days, when I see the procession of happy smiles leaving my clinics, I can hardly believe that there was a time when I wasn't sure that my future lay in dentistry. I've come to realise that it was when I took charge of my career and embraced the business of dentistry that it really became a rewarding profession – one in which I could build up a thriving dental business providing the kind of services I knew people wanted, and expand to offer them on a much larger scale.

It hasn't been plain sailing – I've had lots of setbacks along the way, but also strokes of good fortune, not least opportunities that I've created for myself. If you're at a crossroads in your dental career, trying to decide on your next move, this book will challenge you to think differently.

I was born in a small village in Punjab, India. Both of my parents were teachers, so there was always an expectation that I would go into some kind of profession, but which? Engineering? Medicine? My brother had gone into engineering, so I almost seemed destined to go into medicine – except it just didn't appeal to me.

Dentistry was different. I had a massive accident when I was really young and broke a couple of front teeth. That meant endless visits to the dentist with my father, but I was impressed with the way the dentist looked after me and replaced my teeth, after which I could just get on with my life again. Though I didn't realise it at the time, that was a turning point. I chose dentistry.

My dental education took place in a private dental school in Maharashtra (a state in India). After I qualified, I went back home, but having experienced life in the big city of Mumbai, I found it hard to settle down in a small town. First of all, I went to teach aspects of dentistry in a college near my town, but I knew after a couple of months that this was not for me, so I left and went to Chandigarh, the capital of Punjab.

I lost my way a bit after that: I failed to get on to a Master of Dental Surgery (MDS) course, so I returned home, but was unable to get my old teaching post at the dental college back. I didn't know what to do. Though my parents were supportive, they quite rightly pointed out that I couldn't keep on drifting around, trying this and that and not sticking with anything.

My father's solution was to suggest marriage. Soon after that, he introduced me to his friend's daughter, who was visiting India from the UK. I hadn't had any plans to leave India, but after a few meetings, we decided to get married. Within six months, I found myself starting on a new life in the UK in 1998 – and I didn't speak a word of English! This meant I couldn't even ring up the General Dental Council and find out how the English dental system works.

My wife Rita was amazing – she was my rock. She accepted that it would take me time to establish myself. Eventually, I decided that I would just get a job – any job – so that I could be working. That's how I ended up working in a factory printing labels for cardboard boxes, earning £3.20 an hour.

I might still be there if it weren't for my wife going for a routine check-up with her GP. In passing, he asked her about her husband. He was furious to hear that a qualified dentist was working in a factory and put me in touch with a dentist he knew. Now a good friend and mentor, this dentist arranged for me to join a practice as a dental nurse, and looking back, I still think the day that I started there was one of the happiest of my life. Even the high-pitched sound of the drill and the strong smells of the dental materials excited me.

One of the dentists working there was from Pakistan. He had started out as a dental nurse and gone on to qualify as a dentist, showing there was a way forward. From then on, my routine involved long days: I would work in the practice from nine till five-thirty, then get a bus into town to study at the dental hospital library from six till eleven, when the library closed.

I passed the first part of my exams and was excited to be getting nearer to my goal. The second part of the course involved a lot of practical work. I collected extracted teeth and mounted them in plaster of Paris, and I used this model to practise my techniques after the clinic had closed for the evening. Eventually someone advised me that if I really wanted to pass the final exams, I would need to give up my job temporarily so I could focus on my studies.

I did that, took my exams – and failed. That was tough.

Thankfully, my previous employer said to me, 'Don't worry, man. You can start your nursing role again tomorrow', and that's what I did. Without telling anyone – particularly my wife, who was pregnant at the time – I enrolled for the exam again, and this time I passed, rejoining my original practice as an associate dentist.

Perhaps I thought I had wasted a lot of time, but I felt a real sense of urgency to have my own practice. I was approaching the age of thirty and I was fed up with being supported by my wife and having little money to my name.

I bought my first practice in 2003. Thankfully, a bank manager was willing to back me and lent me virtually all the money I needed to buy it. It was a big loan, but I felt I had nothing to lose. I knew I couldn't afford to fail this time, so I put in the hours needed to make the practice succeed.

It seemed as if every month, I was adding a surgery or hiring a dentist or another member of staff. By 2006, I had quadrupled the size of the business. My colleagues and I never turned patients away – if someone turned up in pain, we would promise to see them by the end of the day. We started staying open through lunchtime, because we'd often reopen the surgery in the afternoon to find twenty people waiting outside. Today, it's one of the biggest National Health Service (NHS) practices in Birmingham.

Back when I started the practice, there were only fees per item for dental services; there were no units of dental activity (UDAs). In other words, we were paid for every piece of work we did, but in 2006, UDAs were introduced. Overnight, the scope for growth disappeared and I realised I needed to explore options beyond general dentistry.

A dental business coach put me in touch with a private dentist in London, who generously spent half a day taking me to various practices. This was a real eye-opener. I saw a completely different side of dentistry.

As a result, I opened my first private practice, New Street Dental, in the centre of Birmingham, retaining my original practice as an NHS one. It was at this point that I first heard about Invisalign, a virtually invisible teeth straightening treatment that is custom-made for each patient. I decided to give it a go with a few patients, and was astounded at the results I got, and how quickly.

From then on, things took off. By 2010, I had six practices, then I opened another one in Manchester in 2012. As part of opening yet another clinic in 2014, I took a really close look at my figures and realised how much of my revenue was down to Invisalign. On that basis, I made a decision that was obvious to me, but apparently not to anyone else: I would run a dedicated Invisalign-only clinic. It made perfect sense, because consumer brand awareness was so high that patients were asking for Invisalign by name.

It wasn't long before Align Technology sent someone from its Amsterdam headquarters to visit the clinic. Between us, we explored the possibility of creating a platform on which I could share all my years of experience and expertise – by this time, I was doing 300–400 cases a year – and help other dentists grow their

Invisalign business. I had to put together a concept and business plan, which became the MiSmile Network.

I shared my plan and, in collaboration with Align Technology, made the plan a reality. I was soon travelling the country, introducing the concept to practices interested in expanding into Invisalign. It was well received, but it was a bold move nonetheless. I was asking people to make a significant financial commitment up front, in the form of a joining fee, as well as an ongoing payment, without any proof of the strategy I was selling, but it worked. Of the first twenty practices I visited, twelve are still part of the MiSmile Network. The network now comprises more than one hundred independent dental practitioners located across the UK.

As I was keen to spread the MiSmile message as widely as possible, I developed the MiSmile Academy, a twelve-week online training programme open to all general dental practitioners (GDPs) who would like to grow their Invisalign business. Little did I realise when I started how essential this online training would become. When Covid-19 struck, my plans were well advanced, and in early 2021 the first cohort of MiSmile academicians began their journey.

In January 2022, I launched my first fully immersive training experience – Mastering your Invisalign Business. Each month I invite ten ambitious general dentists to join me to learn the secrets to my Invisalign business success.

Your turn to grow

There comes a point when even the most committed dentist stops and asks, 'What next?' Perhaps you've grown your practice to the maximum size possible for your present location. Perhaps you'd like to branch out into innovation, but are not sure where to start. You may well have considered offering more cosmetic treatments, but the array of brands out there makes it difficult to choose the best option.

Over the course of this book, I'm going to show you how you can take that leap and reach the next level. It won't be a leap in the dark as we'll be following the approach that I've refined over many years, based on Invisalign technology which is consistently reliable. The first part sets out five pillars that have provided the firm foundation for my business growth. In the second part, we'll examine the fundamentals of marketing, finance, clinical confidence and the all-important patient journey.

I've charted my journey in detail and distilled the experience I've acquired over the last fifteen years. I hope you will find the resources in the book – and online – useful and the case studies encouraging.

PART ONE
THE MISMILE WAY

1
Growing MiSmile

When I first opened my practice at New Street, Birmingham, I didn't have many patients, so I advertised and marketed to generate business. A dentist from London heard that a new practice had opened in the Midlands and arranged to come and visit me.

After he'd looked around and spoken to me about the practice, he said, 'Can I hire a room in your surgery for one day a week? I'll pay you whatever you want.'

When I asked him what services he would offer in his surgery, he told me he wanted to do something called Invisalign. That was the first I had ever heard of it. I told him I would have a think about his proposition, but as soon as he left the surgery, I went straight on to Google and typed in the word 'Invisalign'.

I wanted to understand what Invisalign was all about, because as far as I could tell, not many dentists were using it. This quick and convenient way of aligning people's teeth seemed promising. When I looked at the courses the parent company Align Technology was offering, I realised there was one with places available on days that I was free, running in a couple of weeks' time.

When I attended the course, I took with me photographs of patients I thought Invisalign could help. As soon as I got a chance, I sat down with some of the clinical team and showed them the photographs.

'Do you think I could treat cases like these with Invisalign?' I asked. The clinical lead was sure I could and gave me detailed advice, and so it was that I took on my first four Invisalign patients. This was in 2007.

When these four patients came back for their review appointments, I knew I was on to something: they were really happy. Their teeth were moving exactly as we had planned and it had all been so straightforward. I was amazed: orthodontics has a reputation as a complex specialism in dentistry, yet this simple Invisalign device was doing the job effectively with the minimum of intervention.

It was one of those lightbulb moments. I thought, 'You know what? I love this. This is what I'm going to do from now on.' Other dentists were offering a whole raft of services; there were even a couple of dentists in Birmingham doing Invisalign, but they weren't taking it seriously. I was; I'd got the bug and I loved everything about Invisalign.

Once I'd made the decision that it was what I wanted to focus on, I gave Invisalign my all. I went on every webinar, travelled to attend Invisalign summits all over the world, and met people and networked with them to find out how they were making a success of Invisalign. I learned all there was to know about marketing it, about the patient journey and how to set up the treatment plans correctly.

Invisalign's parent company offered a significant discount if a dentist signed up to do eighty cases. It was a big commitment, but I took the plunge. I needn't have worried; in 2008, I did nearly 100 cases, and from then on, my Invisalign practice took off. I wanted to take it to a different level, so I opened a clinic in House of Fraser in Birmingham, followed by similar clinics in Solihull and Manchester. I also opened two more NHS clinics.

The graphic below summarises my evolving approach to growing the business from its beginnings until the present. Apart from the rapid growth, one of the first things you're likely to notice about it is how analogue means of marketing and communication have been completely supplanted by digital channels over the years that I've been in this business. The learning and development never stop, whether the technology is digital or dental – or both.

2007	7 cases	My passion for Invisalign was ignited	Advertising was mainly *Yellow Pages* and local newspaper adverts
2014	260 cases	By now I was focusing my business on Invisalign	I began investing heavily in digital advertising, tested radio and ran open days
2018	460 cases	My success now was built on understanding and communicating my unique selling points – what made me different	My advertising spend at this point was 100% digital
2020	550 cases	I integrated an end-to-end digital patient journey	I put a focus on lead management, integrated video consultations and adopted new digital channels to improve my patient experience

The evolving journey of Invisalign at MiSmile

A new name

By 2014, consumer awareness and demand had reached unprecedented levels, and I was doing

300–400 Invisalign cases a year. Rather than ringing up to make an appointment for a consultation for teeth straightening, people were ringing up to ask for Invisalign by name. That's when I took the bold decision to change my New Street dental practice to a new brand: MiSmile. The MiSmile Invisalign-only clinic.

It was a big step. I'd been in touch with the team at Align Technology, so they knew what I was planning to do, but even so, someone from head office in Amsterdam came over to visit me.

'Sandeep, how do you do it?' he asked.

'It's my trade secret,' I replied. 'Why would I tell anyone else about it?'

He came back with an interesting suggestion. 'Why don't we create a platform together through which you can help other dentists to adopt and grow Invisalign? In return, Align Technology will make sure that this is a commercially viable model for you.'

That was the start of the MiSmile Network, endorsed and supported by Align Technology. This collaboration is now one of the largest general dental practitioner networks in the world. It is in effect an alternative form of franchising, because the dentists running these practices retain ownership of their businesses, make their own decisions and keep their individual names, followed by 'part of the MiSmile Network'.

They pay me a fee in return for my help to grow their Invisalign businesses.

The network has been operating for over seven years now, and three of the members who were only doing about five to ten Invisalign cases a year have now become Diamond Providers, which is the accolade that Align Technology awards to those who are doing more than 150 Invisalign treatments annually. Even though they have achieved this, they still see the value of being part of a network.

CASE STUDY: A SATISFIED MEMBER

Dr Indy Singh is owner and principal dentist at Cathedral Dental in Bury St Edmunds. Here's what he has to say on the subject of the MiSmile Network.

'Joining the MiSmile Network back in 2015 was probably one of the best business decisions I ever made. Initially, my main goal was simply to treat more Invisalign patients. I wasn't really sure how many more; I just recognised the commercial opportunity that the treatment provided – not to mention that I loved treating my patients with Invisalign (and still do).

'I'd heard Sandeep speak at an Align conference and joining the network gave me the push I needed to grow. I never imagined I'd still be a member now, benefiting from the programme as much as I am.

'This year, my team and I were delighted to reach Diamond Provider status – something I never thought we'd achieve. I'm so proud of the team, but also grateful for the ongoing support and encouragement from MiSmile. I don't think we'd ever have got here without them (or at least not as quickly). Even though I know we probably could "go it alone", there are too many advantages to continuing to work alongside MiSmile – the lead generation, the patient journey support and the treatment planning service to name just a few.'

I deliberately designed the programme to support growth for Invisalign dentists, regardless of their size or ambition.

Six years on, there are more Invisalign providers in the UK than ever, but I still want to help as many people to grow their Invisalign business as possible, because that's my passion and it's what I'm good at. This is the inspiration for *Mastering Your Invisalign Business*.

Barriers to growth

Despite the number of dentists who have been able to build successful practices based on Invisalign, there are still some who are either reluctant to adopt the product and its technology or not seeing the growth that they had hoped for. Let's have a look at the main obstacles standing in their way.

Invisalign is for orthodontists

Many dentists see Invisalign as an orthodontic treatment that should only be undertaken by a specialist orthodontist, but this could not be further from the truth. Invisalign is everyday dentistry. It can be part of every dentist's repertoire, something that they routinely offer to suitable patients.

Ten million satisfied patients across the globe are proof that Invisalign is a safe and successful treatment.

Lack of commitment

Some dentists don't follow through with Invisalign. They go on the course, receive their certification, do a couple of cases, and then nothing further. Perhaps they get their fingers burnt through selecting the wrong patients to treat, or perhaps they feel the whole process is taking too long.

For those who make poor selections, my message would be to learn to walk before you can run. If you are just starting out with Invisalign, go for the simple cases. Once you build your confidence, you can gradually take on more and more complex ones. Just because you've done an Invisalign course, it doesn't mean that you can come back to your practice and treat all-comers straight away.

Anyone embarking on something new needs to expect some sort of learning curve, and that takes time. Rest assured that you will always have Invisalign's technology and support behind you while you build up your own expertise and experience to get the most out of the system.

Glass ceiling

Some dentists may be doing two to five Invisalign cases a month, but they don't know how to get beyond that. I can't stress enough that smashing this glass ceiling requires some extra effort and outlay.

If this describes you, perhaps you need to get to grips with digital marketing and raise awareness of your clinic. Be prepared to open earlier and/or close later to accommodate the extra patients you hope will respond to your advertising.

Imitations

There are clear aligner systems out there that are cheaper than Invisalign, but Invisalign is the best – the Rolls Royce. Invisalign's competitors have made many dentists wonder if they can make savings, but a cheaper system will probably take longer to complete the treatment, which is likely to threaten the viability of their business. The average length of time for an Invisalign treatment is about nine months.

Align Technology has invested heavily in research and development, innovating constantly and bringing out modified versions of the Invisalign clear aligner every year. People come into my surgeries saying, 'Can I have Invisalign?' not 'Can I have clear aligners?' Why would you want to miss out on that brand awareness?

A genuine partnership

Even though Align Technology is a massive company, its approach – and mine – is all about people. I still speak regularly to individuals across the company, from a territory manager in a particular location to the senior vice president. We work together with mutual respect and Align Technology has my undivided loyalty. Though I have been courted by other companies, I am committed to the product Align has to offer, its supporting services and way of working.

When a new dentist joins the MiSmile Network, neither my brand nor Align benefits until that dentist takes on a case, so it's in our interests to send them as many leads as we can. It's also in our interests to train them as well as we can. We set up effective Clin-Checks – short 3D animations that allow the dentist to see the predicted Invisalign treatment result before they even begin, so they can continue to learn and take on increasingly complex cases. In fact, you could describe the MiSmile model as a win-win-win for

Align, the MiSmile Network and the dentist. Actually, make that win-win-win-win, because you need to include the end user: the happy, smiling patient.

Having looked at the evolution of the MiSmile Network in this chapter, we'll focus in detail in the next on the specific approaches that have enabled MiSmile's growth and ensured its sustainability. It's these approaches that led me to develop my tried-and-tested MIWAY model, which is what we will go on to examine in detail later in Part One.

2
Developing MIWAY

In this chapter, we will explore the principles and practices that led me to develop the MIWAY model. Then the rest of Part One will look at each stage of MIWAY – mission, image, wow your patients, action and you – dedicating a chapter to each one so we can examine it in detail.

Mindset

You can probably divide the world into two types of people: those with a fixed mindset and those with a growth mindset. People with a growth mindset have a willingness to learn and adapt to new ways of doing things, and will make the most of the systems and support on offer to them.

It was a growth mindset that spurred me on to set up my own practice as soon as I was qualified to do so, but as you may have realised, this mindset was enhanced when I saw what was possible with Invisalign. Once I understood what I could achieve by integrating Invisalign into my day-to-day business, I bought into it wholeheartedly. I knew it would entail keeping up with frequent changes of technology and adopting new practices, and I was up for that.

Don't get me wrong here: I am not suggesting that everyone must have a growth mindset. I have a number of successful associates in my business who love doing dentistry, love the nine-to-five, but don't want the headache of running their own business and have no desire to develop their business acumen. It's about making choices that work for you and doing the type of work that suits what you want out of life.

It's perfectly possible to develop a growth mindset even if you don't have one to begin with. If you feel it's not your natural way of thinking, you can start out with small steps – setting, for example, a modest target for increasing Invisalign cases. Once you've achieved that, you'll probably find you have the appetite to go for a bolder target the following year.

The following graph shows the growth of my practice over fourteen years, and highlights the possibilities with a growth mindset.

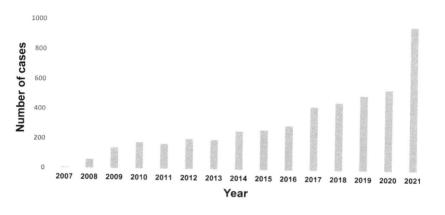

Invisalign growth

CASE STUDY: EMBRACING CHANGE

Here's what Dr Mumta Jilka, principal dentist at Abbey House Dental Practice, Staffordshire, experienced when she and her team bought in to MiSmile.

'We joined the MiSmile Network to grow our Invisalign case volume. To begin with, we hadn't really considered how much we'd need to challenge and change our mindsets. We believed we could keep doing what we'd always done, and MiSmile would slot in around us and help us do more cases.

'It wasn't quite as simple as that. We soon recognised that we needed to embrace some changes and worked with the MiSmile team to adopt a different mindset – a growth-focused approach. Although we made some mistakes along the way, we learned and adapted, and I'm so proud of our practice now.'

Successful innovation

Deep down, do you actually believe in innovation? If you're quite happy with the way things have been going, it can be tempting to stay in your comfort zone and not confront a degree of risk and a steep learning curve.

Even the most reluctant innovator will find that they have to move with the times in the profession of dentistry. It's not as though dentists practise in complete isolation; patients will demand innovation even if dentists are unwilling to embrace it. After all, they talk to one another and are exposed to consumer and social media, so many patients are well informed.

Listening to your patients is vital. You need to gain a deep understanding of what they are looking for, appreciate their concerns and develop empathy with them before you can successfully offer them innovative solutions. It's not enough just to have clinical skills; successful communication with patients is an art in itself. Only once they have trust in you and your practice will they be willing to embrace new techniques.

You also need to bring staff along with you on your journey of innovation. Whether you are a principal or an associate with a desire to adopt innovation, you are in effect in a leadership role. You must have a clear vision for your practice and be able to communicate it to your colleagues in a compelling way.

Obviously, they want to be paid fairly. Career prospects may well be important to them too, but team members are also likely to be keen to feel that they are contributing to the practice; that they are part of a joint enterprise. Before embracing any innovation, put yourself in their shoes and see what the future looks like from their perspective. Once they share your vision and understand the benefits it offers them, they will come on board with you and do whatever they need to do.

Even as an early adopter, I understand that you have to be assured of the quality and effectiveness of any innovation before committing yourself to it, and that there has to be evidence the claims made for it are proven. Let's take the example of Apple. I've been an Apple user all my adult life, because I have a belief in the company and its products. As soon as I hear that Apple is launching a new phone or some other product, I trust in the quality of it, because I feel aligned with the ethos of that company. I don't need to read hundreds of reviews before going out and buying the product.

The same thing applies when it comes to Invisalign. I understand the values and the vision of Align Technology and, by extension, its Invisalign product. This is why I never have any second thoughts about adopting new Invisalign technology. I just go with it, because that course of action has been beneficial for me and my business over the past fifteen years – and for colleagues in the MiSmile Network too.

Planning for innovation

When I say I 'just go with it', I don't mean to suggest that I rush into Invisalign innovations blindly. Any innovation needs to be taken on with a clear understanding of the additional time and money I am going to have to invest to implement it, and the same is true for you. Break down your big overall goals for annual growth into smaller quarterly or monthly goals, so that you can get a handle on and track your return on investment closely.

To take a practical and relevant example, let's look at the option of buying an iTero scanner – a digital scanner to produce colourised images of the teeth and gums. Nowadays you can spread the cost of a scanner over five years with interest-free finance, and one extra Invisalign case a month would cover the cost of that repayment. Most people will find that with the help of the scanner, they can actually do at least three to five extra cases per month.

This reverse engineering – working on the basis of the number of additional cases you estimate you can do every year if you take on new innovation – is a sound way to plan and ensure that you will be able to meet the costs of the innovation. It's certainly preferable to saving up for big-ticket items, thereby delaying innovation in your practice.

In terms of return on investment, I start from a simple premise. If a proposal or opportunity lands on my desk, I ask myself if I am likely to make 10% on my outlay. If the answer is yes, I'll go for it without hesitation, but if it's not likely to make 10%, I need to look at the worst-case scenario. What's the smallest return it might yield?

If you're not even going to get a return of 3% on your investment, it's not worth considering. And if it's somewhere between 3% and 10%? Then it's down to you to examine your beliefs and decide whether you think it's a venture that you can make work.

The MIWAY model

Over the last fifteen years, I have travelled around the world and met many successful Invisalign doctors. During my conversations with them, I've realised that they all had a different journey and those who had reached Align's Diamond status had done so in their own way. The bottom line is that we can all share ideas with each other and learn from what others have done, but we can't copy other people and hope we will achieve similar results. We have to carve out our own path to success.

The MIWAY model that I have developed won't tell you what you should do. Instead, it will show you how to:

- Find your own way of thinking

- Organise your thinking about where you are now

- Plan your journey to Diamond level and take the steps to achieve it

It will encourage you to go deeper into your head to find the answers, so you can carve out your own path to reach your Invisalign growth goal.

The MIWAY model has evolved through my personal experience of offering Invisalign in my clinics over the past fifteen years. During this time, I experimented with lots of ways of marketing, training and creating

Doing It MIWAY model

the ideal patient journey. I was keen to devise, for my own benefit, a dashboard system that would give me instant access to my business performance and identify where things could be improved. I've found over the years that the difference between good and great Invisalign providers lies in the little things that give a service an edge.

Reflection on my own preferences and aspirations, allied with close analysis of 'what works', brought me to the five pillars that form the bedrock of my practice.

These five elements encapsulate both the mindset and the practicalities that need to underpin your Invisalign journey. They give you an overview of what the journey entails, but they're also useful as checklists or reminders along the way as your business expands. If the future ever seems exciting, but a bit overwhelming, the MIWAY model will bring you back to the fundamentals and give you clarity.

The first question I ask myself when anyone wants to join the MiSmile Network is, 'Are they a good fit?' In other words, do they have the right vision? Do their beliefs and values align with ours? In terms of practicalities, do they have the right team structure in place? If not, are they willing to adopt new ways of doing things?

As long as you have a growth mindset and willingness to learn, the MIWAY model and the MiSmile Network can make Invisalign work for you. If you're with me so far, I'm guessing you do indeed have a growth mindset and an appetite for change. The next logical step is to create the conditions for successful expansion through Invisalign.

Let's start off by exploring the first stage of MIWAY: your mission.

3
Mission

In business, the mission is behind everything that an organisation does and the mission statement is vitally important to any organisation with success and growth in mind. It is used to define the purpose of the organisation, inform stakeholders, enable strategy development and identify metrics.

Put simply, the mission of a business is the reason that it exists. To create an effective mission statement for your business, though, you need to be clear on its purpose. There are five questions that help define your business purpose in your own terms:

- Who are you (business-wise)?

- What do you do?

- Who do you do it for?

- Why do they want or need it?

- How will it change their life?

By connecting the answers to these five questions, you can create your own mission statement.

If I were to describe my mission statement at the moment, it would go something like this:

> I am a dentist sharing proven growth prin-
> ciples with other dentists who are driven
> to build up their dental practices through
> the adoption of Invisalign technology and
> promote effective business practices to secure
> a successful future and the fulfilment of their
> dreams.

In this mission statement, everyone benefits. The dentists achieve the expansion they are aiming for, their teams become part of a thriving practice and the patients get the smiles they've always wanted – and it's good for my business, too.

In working out what your mission statement is, bear in mind that it is not necessarily set in stone. To continue doing the same thing you've always done, but more of it, may not be the answer. You need to recognise that there are times when your mission statement may no longer be fit for purpose.

Be alive to the external factors that, despite your own experience and expertise and your commitment to innovative technology, may have a bearing on your practice and who you are providing services for. For example, is your practice in an area that is becoming popular with families with school-age children? Perhaps include training in and taking on the provision of Invisalign Teen in your mission statement. Conversely, if you're practising in an area with an ageing population, your mission needs to keep pace with their increasing need for dental implants and other corrective treatments.

Setting your GOAL

I have always wanted to know where I'm going and what the journey will look like. I often use the analogy of driving a car. It's not enough for me to have the destination and a satnav; I want all the information on the dashboard, such as the amount of fuel I've got, the speed I'm going at, the temperature outside the car as well as the temperature I've set in the car, the volume at which the stereo is playing. This is why I take a methodical approach in my business, building up a step-by-step plan that looks at everything that will get me to my destination.

This probably explains why I didn't like working as an associate – I wasn't in control of the type of dentistry I did or the practice I wanted to create – and why I lost no time in going on a 'How to Set Up Your Dental Practice' course as soon as I was qualified to do so. Setting up my own practice meant I was able to make an independent decision to adopt Invisalign when I had established for myself how effective it was.

If you're an associate, you will have to make the case for Invisalign to your principal. My aim is to provide evidence so compelling that it will be easy for you to do so. I've devised the GOAL model to highlight the factors that will help you to have a clear direction and understand how you can go about following it.

- **G**rowth – what is your ambition?
- **O**pportunity – consider challenges and risks alongside the benefits.
- **A**mbition – plan for the benefits you want to realise.
- **L**earning – what do you need to know?

Growth

Let's take my own experience as an example. Once I'd resolved, following the success of my first four Invisalign cases, to do at least 100 cases a year, I had to sit down and figure out a strategy for how to achieve this and the tactics to support that strategy.

Obviously things changed as I went along: some things worked and some things didn't. I ran with the ideas that were working, doing more and more of those, and I learned from the things that didn't work, moving on to try different approaches.

Before embarking on any journey, you need to sit down with a pen and paper and define what your end point looks like. Then you can be sure that you're continuing on the right trajectory. When new MiSmile members join the network, I encourage them to have a realistic view of what their goal looks like. A modest goal might be a good starting point, but the goal itself is not the only thing to decide on. It's all very well to resolve that you want to do 100 cases of Invisalign a year, but what will that entail? How much time are you prepared to devote to this project? When do you want to achieve this goal by?

You also need a good idea of the type of business you aspire to create. Do you want a lifestyle business or a corporate business? With a lifestyle business, you would aim to build a small clinic, but with a luxury environment and a reputation for being the best for Invisalign in your area. Alternatively, you could make your Invisalign practice part of a 'mixed economy' and develop a clinic focusing on one or two treatments, say Invisalign and dental implants, while the associates in your practice handle the day-to-day routine of check-ups and practical dentistry.

A third possible model is to have a large practice or several practices run by associates who also do the clinical work, while you simply manage the business, which is what I do. If this is your choice, you may need to upgrade your business skills – I certainly spend a lot of time listening to business podcasts or audiobooks and reading relevant material.

CASE STUDY: COMPLEMENTARY PARTNERS

Dr Sam Hainsworth, partner at Smile Stylist, talks about how his strengths and mine complemented each other to form the ideal business partnership.

'I started working with Sandeep back in 2015 as an associate dentist at Smile Stylist, House of Fraser in Manchester. Although I love all aspects of dentistry, my real passion is cosmetic dentistry, in particular Invisalign. Sandeep provided an ideal opportunity for me to work alongside him in a practice that was focused on Invisalign treatments.

'As the years passed, Sandeep took a step back from clinical work and focused his time on running the business. This created the ideal scenario for me to lead the clinical side of the practice. A few years later, when it became clear that we both shared a goal and vision for the practice, Sandeep provided me with yet another opportunity – to become his business partner.

'Smile Stylist now has beautiful new premises in the heart of Manchester in which to thrive. While Sandeep continues to be involved in the overall growth strategy, as clinical director, I am responsible for the day-to-day running of the practice.'

None of the models I have mentioned in this section is necessarily right or wrong for you. None is better than any other; it's just a matter of being clear about what you want, planning accordingly and following through on those plans, all the while making sure your associates understand your aspirations. Above all, you need to be willing to change when you can see that it's necessary to do so.

Opportunity

Dentistry may be your profession, your aspiration may be to create dazzling new smiles, but make no mistake: you are running a business. Whatever you do is going to have an impact on your professional career, your team and ultimately your family. What Invisalign offers is an opportunity to develop your practice into a successful business based on a tried-and-tested service with a strong reputation.

Anything we do has both a positive and a negative impact. One negative impact of working towards the goal of undertaking an increased number of Invisalign cases is that you will have to devote a certain amount of time to it. There is no getting away from the fact, so you need to start planning what this whole enterprise will look like.

Sit down and allocate time specifically to the various activities that increasing your Invisalign caseload will entail, be they marketing, administration or actual dental work. For some people, these time constraints can be overwhelming, so it's important to understand yourself and your circumstances well enough to recognise if such an undertaking is not for you. I certainly don't want to suggest that everyone needs to be goal-driven and ambitious; I just want you to be clear about what the consequences of increasing your Invisalign caseload will be.

If you would prefer to have an easy nine-to-five life, that's your decision to make. Just be aware that if you're not adopting technology, if you're not keeping up with current research and innovation, sooner or later, you will lose relevance in the marketplace. You will not be providing the services that customers are looking for, so they will seek out your competitors.

If you are confident you can take on the challenge and the time commitment needed to increase your Invisalign caseload, you can break through, improve your performance and achieve your goals. Successfully enlarging your Invisalign practice will, of course, mean building a reputation in your area as an expert and all that that entails: growth through referrals and word of mouth; the satisfaction from focusing on one discipline; seeing your skillset improve; and don't forget the happy patients.

Ambition

Where are you heading? Build a clear picture of your destination, and for that you will need to have all the information up front so that you can 'reverse engineer' your plans as you go along.

Let's take a look at a worked example, based on doing 100 Invisalign cases a year.

- A patient pays £3,500 per case: this gives a turnover of £3,500 × 100 = £350,000.

- Once you deduct Invisalign's laboratory costs (this will depend on the level of your discount and your mix of case types), let's say you will be left with £240,000 as gross profit.

- Next, you need to deduct your staff and running costs, your variable running costs, and your rent and rates. This is likely to leave you with around £120,000 as a profit margin.

Basically, you can divide your revenue from Invisalign into three, with one-third going to Align Technology for lab fees, one-third going to cover your expenses, and one-third being your profit margin if you are the principal and are treating these patients yourself.

These raw figures illustrate one possibility, but much will depend on your circumstances and the extent of your personal ambition. For example, are you a principal or an associate? Do you just run the practice or do you do clinical work yourself? In my own case, I run my practices, but no longer do any clinical work myself. This alters the figures in the formula slightly, but the principle is the same.

No matter what stage you're at in your dentistry career, you need to have an eye on your exit strategy. When you're ready to sell your business, what will it look like to a prospective buyer? How will they value the practice that you are running?

To give you a rough estimate of the impact on your exit strategy of reaching your Invisalign goal, I can tell you that dental practices with thriving Invisalign clinics are selling at six to seven times earnings before interest, taxes, depreciation and amortisation (EBITDA). Let's look at how that formula works with our previous example:

$$£120,000 \text{ net profit} \times 7 = £840,000$$

This whole enterprise is starting to make sense, isn't it? How about if you did 200 cases a year?

Once you've identified your ambition, you need to calculate what it represents in terms of turnover, gross profit and net profit. These are just a few broad pointers, as we'll be examining the financial aspects of expanding your practice with Invisalign in detail in Chapter 11.

Learning

Anyone engaged in a career in the medical and allied professions has in effect signed up for lifelong learning, since these fields are advancing all the time. You will always need to strive to improve; the day will never come when you can say, 'I know everything and I can do everything'. If you then decide to develop your practice based on Invisalign, you will add several other subjects to your syllabus:

- **Clinical skills:** patients come to you with a problem and you offer them a solution. You have an ethical duty to offer them the best solution and to treat them in accordance with the highest possible standards. From my fifteen years of experience with Invisalign, I can confirm that it's best to start off with easy cases, gaining expertise and confidence before you move on to more complex ones. Make the most of the ongoing opportunities that Align offers in the form of training sessions, webinars and summits, and never hesitate to reach out to the Invisalign clinical team or to your peers if you have a query or a problem.

- **Business skills:** running a business is a skill, so it's worth spending time learning about it from books or attending courses, but there comes a point when you've got to get out there and try it. Let me tell you, however good you are, there will be times when you will fail. One of the skills of business is to become comfortable with the notion that you will fail at some stage, but this is another opportunity to learn. Sit down with your team and get to the bottom of what went wrong, pinpoint what you could have done differently and devise a plan for what you will do next time.

- **Digital skills:** Invisalign is a treatment predicated on the latest technology. In my opinion, investing in an iTero scanner is a no-brainer. My outlay on the scanner has been repaid ten times over the years. My only regret is that I didn't get one much sooner. While there used to be a time when you could sit back and say, 'Oh, I'm not very IT savvy', you can't get away with this now. There are plenty of people out there who can help you, and if you can learn the clinical skills you need for dentistry, I'm sure you're capable of learning the digital skills. As with most things, it's largely a question of practice.

- **Communication skills:** treat others as you would like to be treated yourself. If you keep that mantra in mind, you won't go far wrong in business. Take time to build up a rapport with your patient, and not just for the sake of it or because it feels good. You need to develop a real connection with them to understand their problem. The more you can empathise with their problem, the more they will open up to you, enabling you to give them a range of options: they can leave everything as is, wear fixed braces, choose Invisalign or have a ceramic plate. Once you've explored all the pros and cons of these options with them, they will feel empowered to make the choice that suits them. What they won't feel is that they've been pressured into something they might regret by a pushy salesperson. A 'sale' will be a natural conclusion to your cordial and constructive meeting with that person.

- **Management skills:** with your clinical, business, digital and communication skills in place, now all you need to do is keep the plates spinning. Businesses need active management to function smoothly and continue to grow, which includes taking care of the boring but vitally important details such as insurance, regulatory compliance, etc, along with managing the premises, the team, the equipment and the systems and processes that drive it. You don't have to do all of this yourself, but you certainly need to know enough about how it's done to maintain oversight of it, and to recognise and recruit an excellent operations team member or practice manager.

Five lessons

Whenever I feel as if I'm getting off track and my purpose seems a bit fuzzy, I always go back and listen to Steve Jobs's Stanford commencement speech.[1] These are the five lessons I take from that speech:

- Much of what Jobs stumbled into by following his curiosity turned out to be invaluable. You can't connect the dots looking forward, but you can do so looking backwards.

- Jobs was fired from his own company, but Apple executives soon called him back. In the meantime, Jobs had started two more companies and both became highly successful. This shows that what seem like the worst of circumstances often lead to the biggest opportunities in life.

- If you want to do great work, you need to do what you love. In his early years, Jobs had to return Coke bottles in exchange for the deposit to buy food, but he persisted and ultimately became a legend because he loved what he did. When you love what you do, your circumstances will not bother you; your passion will give you tremendous strength to keep going until you succeed.

---

1   Steve Jobs's 2005 Stanford commencement address (YouTube, 2008), www.youtube.com/watch?v=UF8uR6Z6KLc, accessed 10 February 2022

- If you don't know what you love, keep looking. Keep exploring and trying new things until you find your passion. People often find it hard to discover exactly what their passion is, and even if they do know what it is, they can't actually find it out there. If you don't find your passion in the world, create it.

- Every morning, Jobs asked himself, 'If today was the last day of my life, would I do what I'm about to do?' If the answer continued to be no for too many days in a row, clearly he was doing something wrong, and this is something we can all learn from. The question then needs to be, 'Why am I not doing what I love?'

After all your reflection and analysis, are you ready to take the next step on the Invisalign journey? Does it align with the mission statement of your business? You've considered both the extra effort and outlay increasing your Invisalign caseload will entail, but will it be worth it? Are you excited at the prospect of enhancing your service to your patients and expanding your practice?

If the answer to these questions is a resounding yes, now it's time to take a close look at the second stage of the MIWAY model: the image of your business. What do you have to offer as a practice and how do you make sure that people are aware of it?

4
Image

One of the first rules of running a business is that your customers, and your potential customers, understand what your business represents. A dental practice is no exception. There are many types of dental practice in Britain and many models of working in the profession, so patients must be able to decide which is right for them.

I developed the ICON model to help you draw out what is unique about your practice, the service you want to offer and you as the leader of it:

- Identity – what your clinic stands for
- Character – your unique features

- **O**rigins – the backstory you bring to your practice

- **N**otice – what sets you apart from the competition

In the UK, the first distinction to be made is between NHS dentistry and private dentistry. Some practices do only NHS work, others do only private work, and some combine both types of dentistry. With a clear mission statement, which we covered in the previous chapter, you will know which type of business works best for you and for what reasons, but if you're considering a change of direction, you need to explore the options open to you. How will external factors – such as location, demographic, competition, etc – have a bearing on them?

Let's have a look at each step of the ICON model in more detail.

Identity

I run several NHS practices as well as private ones. All my private practices are Invisalign focused; everything revolves around Invisalign, so when a patient comes to one of these practices, they already know what it is about. It's clear on all the sources of information that they may have visited, such as websites or social media channels, that Invisalign is what's on offer.

This is one way of differentiating mine from private practices that may offer a mixture of branded services or other types of remedial dentistry, but there are other choices to make when you're considering how to identify your practice. If you are well established in an area with a large group of patients that you have been treating for some time, it may make sense to feature your own name in the name of the practice, for example, the John Smith Dental Practice. This capitalises on your patients' trust and loyalty.

Another option is to base your practice name on your location, for example, Birchfield Dental Practice. This may be especially useful if you are seeking to establish yourself in a particular catchment area. It can also work to your advantage when people are searching online for a dentist in their locality.

An alternative approach to highlighting a branded treatment such as Invisalign in your name is to feature the name of the dental group that you belong to, such as MiSmile or the Smile Birmingham Group. Whichever option you go for, it's important that people have a clear idea of who you are business-wise and what your mission is before they come to the clinic. Delivering a high level of patient satisfaction is vital, as failure to meet expectations, however trivial the reason might be, only leads to customer frustration.

Character

I can't stress enough how important it is to know what you want out of your dental career when you're deciding your next move. There are many points on the scale between ambitious target-driven empire builder and tradition-minded practitioner content to treat the patients who present themselves at the clinic, and there's no 'one size fits all' model to achieve your goals. The only common outcome needs to be satisfied patients with healthy teeth.

Your practice's character

I'm going to assume that you are keen to grow your practice with Invisalign and are up for the effort that it will entail. It's at this stage that you will have to decide to what extent you make your personality part of the offer to your patients and how you will communicate it to them. Think about what sort of welcome you will give those calling your clinic. Will it be 'Thank you for calling MiSmile' or 'Thank you for calling Dr Kumar's Dental Practice'?

This decision may depend to a degree on where you are in your career at the moment. If, for example, you are in the middle of your career and well established in a community where you and the nature of your practice are well-known, it makes sense to trade on your personal identity. Bear in mind, though, that somewhere along the line, you will probably want to pivot to a practice identity that can be handed on more easily. At the point where you want to sell your business, it would of course be more useful to associate it prominently with a recognised brand or group.

No matter how good a reputation you may have as a practitioner, it will be undermined if patients don't feel right when they come into your practice. It goes without saying that a practice needs to be spotlessly clean, tidy and well-organised in its processes. That is the absolute minimum that patients have a right to expect. Beyond this, there are many ways of tailoring your practice to your prospective patients, and most of them have little to do with your professional skills.

Patients visiting a high-end practice will expect a different welcome to the one available from a neighbourhood dentist where the patient is greeted at the front desk and asked to take a seat until their regular dentist is ready. The high-end practices tend to be concierge led, with someone welcoming a patient at the door, sitting them down and bringing them a cup of tea or coffee. They will then offer the patient an iPad so that they can go through the entire prospective journey with them.

CASE STUDY: MISMILE BIRMINGHAM

In 2019, the retail space next to my MiSmile Birmingham flagship practice became available and I took the opportunity to extend the practice from one to three surgeries. Demand for Invisalign in Birmingham was increasing and it seemed sensible to expand the surgery capacity to service the rise in patient enquiries.

Trebling clinical capacity meant I had to consider my internal patient journey and flow, and it was at this time I introduced a concierge-led model. I did away with the traditional reception desk and replaced it with a simple table and stool where the front-of-house team sit, welcoming new and existing patients. There are no computers or ringing telephones, resulting in a quiet and calming atmosphere. In a back office, out of sight and sound of the main waiting area, a new patient coordinator manages leads and enquiries.

This simple shift in patient flow has had a fantastic impact on the practice, not least in providing an exclusive high-end patient experience.

You might want to modify a concierge-led approach in an area with a predominantly elderly population, who may not thank your team for presenting them with an iPad. Often, older people prefer to be talked through the treatment and complete any forms on paper.

Your team's character

The individual characters working in a dental practice matter less than the sum of their parts. By this, I mean that collectively, a group of dentists' output should be an all-encompassing service that meets your particular patients' needs and expectations, each individual bringing complementary skills to the team.

There's no point in having five amazing Invisalign providers in your practice; it would make much more sense for the patients and your business to have three amazing Invisalign providers, someone who is an expert at cosmetic bonding and someone who excels at dental implants.

Build a team that will complement your skills and strengths. In other words, you want a team with BALANCE:

- **B**old
- **A**gile
- **L**eading
- **A**ccountable
- **N**oticeable
- **C**ommitted
- **E**ngaged

As a team, my associates and I live by these qualities. Anyone in business has to be bold, but also agile enough to respond to changing demands. We all lead in our own departments or specialisms, and together we are accountable for the quality of service that the practice provides. We are all noticeable in being committed to getting the best outcome for our patients, and engage with them and our colleagues 100% to support one another in what is a collective effort.

Origins

Being clear about your personal story helps you to build credibility and confidence not only in your own mind, but also with your patients. This is an integral part of my approach when someone comes to me for a consultation.

After sitting down with a patient and initiating a conversation to build rapport, I will ask them how much they know about my business. As the answer is usually 'Not a lot', this gives me the opportunity to set my story and achievements out clearly. I can then build on this to give the patient the assurance that my practices have many happy patients, with many testimonials confirming this. I follow this with a complete breakdown of the package the patient will be buying – what they can expect at every stage of the treatment and the cost – as well as reassurance that their treatment will not be complete until they are satisfied with the results.

If someone doesn't know your story, you are just another Invisalign provider. They may have found their way to your clinic, but you still need to tell them about your unique selling points (USPs), be they convenient opening times, expertise with nervous patients or an on-site scanner that cuts down treatment time. Every individual and every practice has a story to tell, so you need to make yours memorable for patients.

Stories may become a valuable marketing tool for your practice further down the line, when word of mouth can be an effective way of spreading your message and attracting new patients. In fact, the stories that other people tell about you are even more powerful than the ones you tell about yourself, so make sure you capture testimonials and anecdotes from your patients. Telling stories and initiating discussions online are brilliant ways to engage prospective patients, because you can impart genuinely useful information to people while demonstrating your expertise and showcasing your results.

If you are building social capital beyond your business, be sure to tell people about it. In my early years, I had to focus exclusively on achieving certain growth targets, but as the MiSmile business grew, I felt I had a responsibility to help others. I was having a great deal of success, but part of giving people a better smile is helping everyone, so I decided with my team to collaborate with a charity that prioritises smiles as much as we do.

I'm proud of MiSmile's association with Operation Smile. We have raised more than £130,000 in four years for this well-established charity that provides safe surgery for children born with cleft lips or cleft palates all over the world. The practice donates £3 for every Invisalign case it takes, while the MiSmile Network adds an additional £4 to the donation, giving Operation Smile a total of £7. Our aim is to raise £1million.

Whenever I hear the amount MiSmile has raised for the charity so far, I feel a huge sense of accomplishment, and of pride in my fellow dentists. I gave every MiSmile member the opportunity to opt out of the partnership with Operation Smile, but not a single person did. Everyone wants to contribute; they see the impact of our fundraising and want to help, and patients are delighted to hear that through their fees, they are helping to support this valuable work.

Notice

Alongside your story are the hard facts that underpin the service you offer. You could call them standards or guarantees. They may sound mundane compared to the personal elements in your story, but they are vital for building trust in your practice – and trustworthiness is probably at the top of the list of qualities you want to be noticed for.

For the MiSmile Network, there are certain fixed commitments:

- If you contact us, we will get back to you within two hours.

- We will offer you an appointment within seventy-two hours.

- You will have a comprehensive treatment plan before any work starts.

Beyond this, there are variations between practices which may be more relevant to some patients than others. Whatever unique practicalities you can offer, though, you need to make sure people know about them. For example, if you are fortunate enough to have parking at your practice, let people know. Along with your story, these practicalities will make you noticeable and distinct from others.

One key practical area in which you can differentiate your practice from others is in the financial terms you offer. Most people offer twelve months' interest-free finance, but if you are prepared to offer this for twenty-four months, that will certainly distinguish you. You could also offer discounts for payment upfront.

Purple Cow

'What has this got to do with anything?' you may ask. Alternatively, you may recognise *Purple Cow* as the title of Seth Godin's compelling book, subtitled *Transform your business by being remarkable*.[2] When I read

---

2   S Godin, *Purple Cow: Transform your business by being remarkable* (Penguin, 2005)

it, I realised that Align is indeed a company remark-able for having challenged the orthodoxy of the orthodontic approach to teeth straightening through its clear aligners. I decided to build my own iconic brand by standing on the shoulders of giants like Align Technology, and I believe what MiSmile is doing now is unique as a business model in which all parties share the success.

In this chapter, we've explored in detail what you can do to create your own brand and identify your USPs. In other words, we have concentrated on your business's image, the second stage of MIWAY. You may have been doing some or even all of this already, or this may mean a new departure for you, in which case I wish you every success. Either way, I encourage you to reach out to MiSmile if you could do with support along the way.

Now it's time to put the patients under the microscope and look at how you can wow them.

5
Wow Your Patients

To build up any dental practice, you need to have a good idea of the people you want to treat and how to find them. Much will depend on the demographic of the area you are in, and on knowing how to reach out to those who are interested in your services.

If you follow my AIMS model, you will not go far wrong in identifying your prospective patients and treating them well in every sense of the word.

- **A**udience – what is your current patient profile and who do you want it to be?

- **I**magination – how does your target audience think, feel and live?

- **M**arketing – how do you reach your target audience?

- **S**atisfaction – how do you fulfil and even exceed their expectations?

Let's now have a look at each stage of the AIMS model in more detail.

Audience

The Invisalign audience is, of course, a subsection of the total potential audience for a dental practice. In broad terms, the archetypal Invisalign patient is female, twenty-five to thirty-five years old, with disposable income and ambition to succeed in her line of work. She may be the classic Invisalign patient, but beyond her are many other groups eager to take up Invisalign treatment.

It's useful to conduct an analysis of your own patient cohort to see how many of them conform to this profile, so that you can establish how many potential candidates for Invisalign you already have in your practice. That will give you some idea of the extent to which you may need to adapt your practice and reach out to a constituency beyond your usual one.

Location, location, location – a prime location is the key to attracting a wide demographic. It is probably an even more important consideration for setting up a dental practice than it is for buying a house. If you want to be successful with Invisalign, in my opinion, there is nothing better than a city-centre location, surrounded by other service providers and retail outlets. Here is where you will get the highest footfall of the greatest range of people. This is not to say that Invisalign will never work in a suburban practice, but you are unlikely to get the same volume of uptake.

Imagination

Never forget that patients are people. The more you show that you respect them and listen to their concerns, the more enthusiastic advocates for your practice they will become, and the more advocates you will have.

Now is the time to use your imagination to understand where your ideal patients are coming from. Men are catching up with women in being concerned about their appearance, so more of them are opting for Invisalign. The treatment is also more affordable than it used to be, making it accessible to people from all walks of life.

To give you an idea of the range of people seeking Invisalign treatment, I need look no further than my own practice: my oldest patient is in their mid-seventies, and I'm also seeing teenagers and Millennials coming in. All these may only add up to a minority of patients compared to the target audience for my business as a whole, but it's still worth catering for them.

To understand your target audience, you need to be able to put yourself in their shoes and imagine how they think and feel, and what they do. Then you need to pinpoint what the appeal of Invisalign might be for different groups of people. Among the young and image conscious, it will probably be part of an aspiration to a high level of self-presentation. Some in this group may have teeth alignment that many would find acceptable, but the perfectionist will want to improve on this. People in prestigious professional roles will also want to present an image that projects health, being in control and confidence. This is best done with a smile that they are proud to reveal.

Others may have missed out on the orthodontic treatment that many people undergo in their teens and have been desperate to remedy this for some time. Clinically, their cases may be more demanding, but the reward – both for them and for you – is that the transformation can be truly remarkable. For the patient, it can even be life-changing, bringing them confidence and opening up doors and opportunities in a way that they could never have imagined.

All these scenarios are key to crafting messages to prospective patients that will resonate with them.

Marketing

I will be covering marketing in more detail in Chapter 8. Here, I just want to give an overview of it so you can understand how it fits into the formula for wowing your patients in a successful Invisalign practice.

If you have a city-centre practice in a prominent location, prospective patients will be able to find you easily. They are likely to stumble across your premises on their way to work, while shopping or while they are out and about for leisure purposes, but you also need to target your audience through the social media platforms that they use. It's fair to say that even someone who passes your practice every day may still use their smartphone as their first port of call when they're looking for a dentist or Invisalign treatment specifically.

My practices now advertise on all social media platforms, but within that, my team and I make every effort to understand which people are watching on those platforms. What are they aspiring to be? Who are their role models?

Who do you know?

Often, your future business is there in your community. Don't overlook the results you can get simply from talking to the people you have on your books. After all, you have done half the work already: they know you and presumably like your work, otherwise they would not be existing patients. This is the foundation of word-of-mouth business.

Do your current patients actually know that you offer Invisalign and other related services? Do you have any banners or posters that would help you to start a conversation with them about these treatments? When people are already in your clinic, you are in a good position to explain to them directly what the treatment would entail and the financial arrangements they could take advantage of, especially if you've got the technology at your disposal to show them what the end result would look like. Videos of patients who have been through your treatment can be both compelling and reassuring.

When you complete a patient's treatment, ask them whether they are happy with what you have done. I'm prepared to bet they will be delighted with the result, and if they are, they will not mind you asking them to tell their friends and family about your service. You can even give them some business cards to pass on to people they know who might be interested. After all, they have no way of knowing without you telling them that you are accepting referrals. Your busy and popular clinic might look to them as though you couldn't take on any further patients.

What I am not in favour of is offering patients incentives to become your advocates. If someone genuinely values your service, they will be happy to recommend you without any incentive. By all means, if you realise that someone has referred a patient to you, send them some chocolates or a bottle of wine afterwards to show your appreciation, but make sure none of your advocates are motivated by the prospect of a reward.

If your patients sense that you respect them and have their best interests at heart, they will be happy to go to their friends and families with recommendations. This is the result of excellent customer service, so make sure you wow them every step of the way.

A standout offer

Let's imagine you've identified the channels you want to advertise on and who you're aiming to appeal to. What is it that's going to catch someone's eye as they scroll through the mass of messages and images that land on their device every day? What will make them opt for you rather than for your competitor?

This is where you need to think about consumer triggers. There is a range of financial incentives you could offer, such as discounts – if your competitor is doing a £500 discount, could you do £1,000? Could you include free teeth whitening? I'm not saying always compete on price – it may be that your credibility, perhaps confirmed by local people, could be equally persuasive.

Understanding the consumer mindset is vital for getting this standout offer right. For most patients, signing up for Invisalign treatment is a big financial commitment – £3,000 to £4,000 on average – but advertising it for £30 a month over a number of years makes it sound a far more manageable prospect. If you wanted to be even more granular, you could express it as the equivalent of a Starbucks latte every day.

You're not necessarily reducing your prices, just presenting them in a way that sounds more affordable. In doing so, you're also helping the price-conscious to make a calculation as to whether they could fit Invisalign into their monthly budget.

Satisfaction

For many people, it's not so much price as quality that counts. Because dentistry is a regulated profession with rigorous clinical standards that we all have to adhere to, I'm assuming that in the vast majority of practices, the provision of Invisalign, as with all other dental services, will be first-rate.

Beyond quality, it's service that will make your practice stand out for patients. Engaging them as fully as possible right from the start sends the message that you want them to have a rewarding experience with you, so ensure that they know where they can park or what transport they can take to get to you. Likewise, you need to highlight the professional associations you belong to, the guarantees that come with your treatment and any awards you may have received – Invisalign Diamond Status is a prime example.

Following through

When someone's taken the plunge and booked an appointment at your clinic for next week, what do you do next? What you don't do is sit and wait for them to turn up. You've got several days in which to build an enduring relationship with them. When you are on the other side of the equation – that is to say, you are the one with all the clinical expertise and experience – it's easy to underestimate how daunting people can find a trip to the dentist, even if it's for a cosmetic treatment rather than a remedial one.

The simplest way to start is by sending an email or a text telling them you're looking forward to seeing them, perhaps giving them a link to click so they can see the location of the nearest car park and how long it will take to walk from there to the clinic. The more they know what to expect from the visit, even down to how they can get there in the most convenient way, the happier they will be.

You could provide further reassurance by sending them some before and after pictures and testimonials from satisfied customers. All of these approaches from you will show them that you are doing all you can to put them at ease and make sure that their visit will be a comfortable one. In short, you're letting them know that you care about them as well as care for them. This is invaluable for differentiating you from the competition.

CASE STUDY: PUT AT EASE

A MiSmile patient tells how her worries were eased ahead of her first Invisalign appointment:

'I had pondered for months about whether to take the plunge with Invisalign, but I needn't have worried. The staff at the practice were fantastic – so professional and welcoming, addressing every concern I could possibly have before the appointment, making me feel like my custom really mattered to them. They were extremely thorough in the assessment appointment, so I left knowing exactly what I could expect from the treatment.

'I get really nervous in dentist settings, but the MiSmile people made me feel comfortable and certain I was in safe hands. With such great service so far, I'm excited to get further into the treatment.'

Patients are at the heart of everything my business does. If I had to sum up my business model in a few words, I would say, 'We are transforming smiles to change people's lives.' I have focused on developing the whole business around this motto so that I can be sure everyone who walks through the door of my practices will be wowed.

Now you've found your patients and you know how to wow them, how do you go about delivering your service in the best possible way? In the next chapter, we'll look at how to set up your clinic and your teams to offer first-rate Invisalign treatment and ensure winning smiles.

6
Action

This chapter is based on the approach that has worked well for me and my MiSmile colleagues over the years, but you will know best how to shape the service you offer to your community and your prospective patients. As it's the actions of the team members of your practice that are the key to its success, the model for my approach is appropriately summed up by the acronym TEAM:

- Tailored – design the blend of people in your team with the service you want to provide in mind.

- Efficient – the standards and systems in your practice need to allow for a seamless patient experience.

- **A**ccountable – set and agree clear expectations to enable people to work in harmony in their complementary roles.

- **M**onitored – keeping track of the financial and professional health of the practice will ensure there are no nasty surprises.

My aim is to build a great team and look after them so well that they go out of their way to wow MiSmile customers at each step of their journey. With the TEAM in mind, let's have a closer look at each stage.

Tailored

When it comes to building or developing your team, much will depend on your location and the demographic you are serving, as well as your own aspirations. Here, I've set out the optimum approach from my perspective, but you will want to consider how to adapt it to the conditions you are working in.

The ideal Invisalign-focused dental practice will have three clinicians – two full time and one part time. To support them, you need three dental nurses and a part-time hygienist. This represents the full complement of clinical staff.

First contact

There are also a number of non-clinical roles to be filled. As I see it, you need four basic roles to ensure the smooth running of the practice and continuity for the patients:

- A new patient coordinator (NPC)
- A receptionist/concierge
- A treatment coordinator (TCO)/sales and marketing manager
- A practice manager

Each of these individuals needs to have a thorough understanding of their roles and how they interact with one another. For your business to be successful, these colleagues need to work together as if they are in a relay race, seamlessly handing the baton on from one person to the next to ensure the best experience for the patient. I'll explore the patient-facing roles in more detail in Chapter 9.

Let's assume that people are aware of the service you offer and someone has enquired about treatment. The NPC needs to respond to this enquiry within two hours. In general, people have lots of options and not much patience, so if you do not respond quickly, they will simply go elsewhere.

The NPC is the patient's crucial first contact with the practice. Their job is not to provide detailed information about treatments or pricing. They need to build rapport with the patient and bring them in for a consultation.

It's at that point that the prospective patient will meet the front-of-house team member, be it a receptionist or, in some practices, a concierge. This is another opportunity to develop the relationship with them and make them feel comfortable. I'd advise the front-of-house staff to show them round the practice and give them an idea of what to expect when they come for treatment.

Then it's time to pass the patient on to the TCO whose role is to find out what their pain point is and explore what they want to achieve. If the patient's introduction to the practice has been handled in this way, nine times out of ten, they will sign up for the treatment and the TCO can book them in to see the dentist.

The practice manager may remain invisible to patients, but they would certainly notice if nobody was performing this function. The practice manager is not responsible for the revenue or the marketing of the business; their role is to ensure that the business runs like clockwork and the team is working together harmoniously and productively. They check in regularly with team members to ensure that everyone is doing everything properly.

Managing contractors, assuring compliance with Care and Quality Commission requirements and all the administrative work running any business entails are also the responsibility of the practice manager.

The clinicians

Once the TCO has handed the patient on, the first job for the clinician to do is a thorough oral health assessment. There may be some remedial work to be done before Invisalign treatment can start, such as fixing a broken tooth or administering a scale and polish.

It goes without saying that the clinicians need to be highly skilled. They also need to be committed to offering a first-rate service – it's this attitude that I'm looking for when I'm hiring for my practices. I am confident that my associates will be able to train people with basic dentistry skills to provide excellent Invisalign treatment, but alongside this, fitting in to the MiSmile culture is important.

Finding the right people

Whenever I am looking for new MiSmile staff, I tend to use three main portals:

- Indeed – for the non-clinical roles

- Dental Talent – for non-clinical and clinical roles

- BDA (British Dental Association) Jobs – for clinical roles

These partners are good at helping me find the right people, who my team and I will then put through a rigorous recruitment process consisting of two stages – a first interview by the area manager and the clinical director, followed by an interview with me – to ensure we get someone with the right skills and attitude.

We're also keen to give dental assistants opportunities to develop their qualifications further and progress in their careers. Part of the MiSmile appraisal process is to find out about the aspirations of our team members and help them grow. This might be through operational support or financial support, depending on the channel that is right for them.

Efficient

As the leader or principal, you will want to have absolute confidence that you can share the workload of running the practice with your team in a way that makes sense for all concerned. Every team member needs to have a clear understanding of what is expected of them – on a daily, weekly, monthly, quarterly and yearly basis. Well-defined roles mean that people can feel confident when taking up their post that they will fulfil these expectations.

For clinicians, efficiency lies in the quality of their dental work and the level of their customer service. I recommend you review both yearly.

CASE STUDY: CONTINUING PROFESSIONAL DEVELOPMENT

Dr Oliver Smart, clinical director at MiSmile Birmingham, talks about working with my practice to broaden his horizons.

'I was introduced to Sandeep at an Invisalign forum in 2011, and in 2012, after achieving Invisalign Platinum status myself, I approached Sandeep about working together as I felt I had gone as far as I could in my current practice.

'Sandeep was open to this suggestion as he was looking to decrease his own clinical commitments. I became associate dentist in 2012, and in 2013, when the clinic relaunched as MiSmile Birmingham, I became clinical director.

'Over the years, Sandeep and I have developed a close working relationship, which I value greatly. The quality of both my dentistry and my patient manner has strengthened Sandeep's trust in my ability, and in 2015, when the MiSmile Network launched, I became clinical director of the group too.

'Being introduced to Sandeep was one of the best things that has happened to me, professionally and personally.'

Systems

Alongside everyone being clear about their roles and responsibilities, the routines and processes that a practice adheres to will enable it to run smoothly. The DenGro software MiSmile uses provides all the prompts that the team needs both to follow up on prospective patients and to monitor the progress of existing patients through treatment and aftercare.

In terms of clinical procedures, Align's doctor site will take you through the whole process, from registering the patient to uploading the scans and the X-rays, setting out your treatment plan and receiving their confirmation. This platform will also flag updates on products that are due to launch, and forthcoming training opportunities and webinars.

Because in some respects a dental practice is no different from any other business, it's important not to overlook the systems that any organisation needs to have in place if it is to offer a good service to customers and a productive working environment for its staff. These include:

- Regular team meetings

- Regular appraisals

- Health and safety monitoring

- A complaints procedure

Accountable

Any dental practice is clearly accountable to its patients, but it also has a wider accountability to the profession itself to uphold statutory standards for clinical work. As an employer, you are accountable for the actions of your team, but within their areas of responsibility, they are accountable to patients and colleagues.

Good communications are at the heart of accountability. Team members not only need to know exactly what they are expected to deliver, but also who they can go to if there is anything they are not happy with. It's vital that people feel comfortable with raising any concerns they have. This helps you to pick up anything that might be going wrong at an early stage and prevent small issues from developing into serious problems.

The MiSmile team has regular meetings, from the daily morning huddle to more formal quarterly meetings. These provide an opportunity for team members not only to share and keep on top of what's going on in the practice, but also to foster MiSmile's collective approach to responsibility. It's important for clinicians to be able to see beyond their own patient list.

Knowing the boundaries of their roles doesn't mean that people have no discretion to act autonomously. At MiSmile, for example, our sales and marketing manager organises her time in the way she sees fit. As long as my associates and I get the outcome we are looking for at the end of the month, I'm not concerned about how we get there.

Even in clinical roles, there is a degree of leeway. Dentists have their own way of doing things and have trained in different ways, using different materials. As long as they comply with the professional standards and the patient is happy, that's all that counts.

Monitored

Knowing exactly where you stand in your business at any given time is vital. You need to have at your fingertips the information on the number of patients currently undergoing treatment, the income they are bringing in and your expenditure on running the practice.

At one time, my practice used to have a spreadsheet for each and every task: how many leads we were getting; how many consultations we were giving; how much revenue we were generating; and so on. Now, monitoring this information is all done through the DenGro customer management software, which was built around MiSmile and beta-tested on it. It is now available to any dental practice that would like to use it. It's also customisable to suit your particular circumstances.

DenGro generates reports that enable you to track your practice's performance, comparing results month on month, quarter on quarter, year on year. If you have set clear parameters for the number of consultations you expect each month, the number of people you expect to see proceed to treatment and the income that will be generated from that activity, monitoring these parameters closely in this way will enable you to take corrective action quickly.

DenGro also helps to streamline the workload of every member of staff. For example, once the NPC has seen a patient and booked a consultation, they simply click the relevant button and that will launch communications, outlining what the patient can expect at their next appointment. As each team member who uses DenGro ultimately contributes to patient conversion, it's vital that they keep the system up to date and accept accountability for their part in the patient journey.

Every so often, for whatever reason, someone will fail to complete their treatment. Hopefully, this will happen rarely, especially if you have supported them throughout their journey and given them all the information they need when they need it to make their visits to the clinic easy. If you have done all this and still they don't complete, you have to accept that it's just one of those things. At least you will know you have not given them any excuse not to continue with it.

My message to my team is simple: 'Treat our customers as you would like to be treated.' Keep this principle in mind and you will never be too far off track as it will help you to make a right decision 99% of the time. With that right decision, you will then be equipped to take the right actions to ensure everyone who visits your practice leaves with a big smile.

One of the best things about dentistry, in my view, is how much it relies on teamwork. Collaborating every day with trusted colleagues who are committed to quality action that contributes to the output of the practice is a privilege, but you don't have to submerge yourself body and soul in the practice. In the next chapter, we will look at you and why it's important to create some time and space for yourself.

7
You (Are The Answer)

I've chosen 'You' for the last letter of MIWAY because in the end, it's all down to you: your aspirations, your talents and your determination. You can get all the external factors right, but if the project hasn't got the momentum of your personal drive behind it, beware!

This explains why my model for You is SELF:

- **S**elect what you are going to focus on and don't be distracted.

- **E**levate yourself by building on your strengths.

- **L**ead your practice and your team.

- **F**ree yourself to choose how to spend your time.

Let's have a closer look at each point.

Select

It's easy to be pulled in all directions when you are running a business; you can end up trying to focus on so many things at once that nothing really gets the attention it deserves. You need to be able to distinguish between what is important and what is merely urgent, because the two are not the same.

This method of deciding on the priorities for your time has been attributed to US President Dwight Eisenhower and can be explored through a matrix.[3] I've populated the one below with examples from the context of a busy dental practice.

I try to devote 80–90% of my time to the tasks that are important rather than urgent. As Eisenhower observed, there is always something urgent going on, but enticing as it may be to wade in and sort it out, I advise against it. I'm always aware that I need to rein myself in to concentrate on what is vital for the long-term health of the business.

When it comes to identifying priorities, I imagine a triangle with the most important priority at the apex of the triangle. For me, that priority is setting the vision

---

3   'Introducing the Eisenhower Matrix', www.eisenhower.me

for the business. The point of the triangle is supported by two further equal angles at the base – one represents people and the other marketing and finance.

	Urgent	Not urgent
Important	• Handling patient complaints • Having broken equipment repaired • Dealing with internet or server issues • WhatsApp messages • Phone notifications	• Strategy planning for next twelve months • Marketing planning • Training and development • Refining patient journey • Appraisal meetings for staff
Not important	• Phone ringing • Emails	• Writing article for local newspaper on developments in dentistry • Organising team night out

If forced to select between these two, I would always go for people. I spend a lot of time with my teams, in particular with my leadership team. Together, we seek to understand where we are now and what the future looks like. I'm always there for my team whenever they need me. I'm also always part of my team, sitting with them rather than handing down orders.

Once your people are taken care of, you can turn your attention to figures, forecasts and the like.

Saying no

It's natural to want to be adventurous and positive, and to feel that we can take on anything, but we need to be able to identify what to say no to, both in the clinical area and in terms of the business.

Looking back, I can pinpoint a handful of cases that were beyond my experience and expertise, and I regretted having taken them on. In each of them, I was able to redeem the situation by referring the patients on to a specialist, so there was no harm done, but it's vital we all know our limitations and get comfortable with saying no to cases that are beyond those limitations.

When it comes to business opportunities, exercise exactly the same self-discipline. I don't think a day goes by when I don't hear from someone who wants to enter a partnership with me or collaborate in some other way. You have to know your 'true north' and keep it in front of you. I'm not saying close your ears and your mind to every unforeseen opportunity; you need to listen carefully and, before you come to any decision, consider how what is being proposed will fit in with your overall growth strategy. If it doesn't, say no to it. As the saying goes, don't try to chase two rabbits, because you won't catch either of them.

Elevate

You need to give yourself every opportunity you can to grow your business and yourself. The key to that is to know yourself inside out, and to be clear-sighted about what you are good at and not so good at. Once you've identified your weaknesses, find the people for whom these are strengths. By complementing your strengths, they will help you achieve your vision.

I see far too many people who want to be good at lots of things and work on their weaknesses to eliminate them. To my mind, this is a wasted effort; my message is to focus on your strengths and surround yourself with amazing people who are much better than you are at certain things. For example, I work closely with – in fact, I rely on – my strategy director, my operations director and the area manager, as their organisational and administrative skills far surpass mine.

What gets you out of bed in the morning? What works for me are business-focused activities: developing MiSmile's strategy, enhancing its communications, shaping the patient journey. If you build on what you're already good at, you have a head start. Ally this with what really excites you – what gets you out of bed in the morning – and you have a formula for success that goes beyond money. That's what will elevate you and your business to the next level, and then the next.

Staying ahead of the game

I'm assuming that as a dentist, you will already be doing everything you need to do to keep abreast of clinical developments. As Align invests heavily in improving its product year on year, there are always innovations coming through to keep up with. Align provides lots of opportunities to update your knowledge with online learning. It also hosts growth and European summits every year, which I would recommend you attend.

When you're enhancing the business side of your practice, podcasts have a lot to offer. You can be listening to them while travelling or even relaxing. I spend a lot of time listening to business-related podcasts, but not confined to the dental profession. You can develop a bit of tunnel vision if you just focus on your own niche. At the end of the day, business is about people, so much of what you will learn can be applied to any business.

CASE STUDY: MY DAY

Everyone structures their day slightly differently to suit their needs. Although I've always been pretty driven, my routine hasn't always benefited my goals. In earlier years it was very easy to roll out of bed, grab a coffee and a bit of breakfast and straight off to work. Life became fairly mindless – get up, breakfast, work, home, dinner, bed, then start all over again the next day. My routine was not serving me.

In recent years, I have gradually come to understand what works for me and for my goals. My day starts early, before five o'clock most days, with meditation to begin. I find this sets the tone for the day as it gives me the calm and focus needed. I follow this up with journaling – handwritten – ensuring I focus on the positive; looking for things I am grateful for, along with a component for setting goals and reviewing them. This keeps me aligned with my intentions, reminding me what I'm aiming for both in that day and in life overall.

Some form of exercise usually comes next, coupled with listening to a podcast or a book. Exercise helps wake up your body and prepare your mind for the day, and it's a perfect time to take on new ideas and allow your mind to absorb these.

These morning rituals allow me the time to shift my mindset to the positive end of the scale and focus on what is necessary to drive my business, and my life, forward.

Small changes can reap huge benefits; it's all about finding what works for you.

Steven Bartlett's *Diary of a CEO,* in which he talks to entrepreneurs, is a fascinating podcast.[4] He interviews people who have failed as well as high achievers and captures exactly the mindset you need if you are to embark on a future in business. Another podcast I listened to recently is by Toto Wolff, the principal of

4   S Bartlett, 'Diary of a CEO' (Apple Podcasts), https://podcasts. apple.com/gb/podcast/the-diary-of-a-ceo-with-steven-bartlett /id1291423644

Mercedes's Formula One racing team.[5] I found all he had to say about his vision, how he set up his team and how he manages difficult periods so relevant to what I do on a day-to-day basis in my own business.

I'd encourage you to range widely to find out what's happening in medicine, nutrition, sport and the environment, for example, and discover how people in those sectors are elevating their game.

Lead

First and foremost, leadership is not about setting the direction for your business, and then telling your team to go out and make it happen. It's more like 'This is where I think we should be going. Tell me what you think and let's go there together.'

The stronger the engagement from all parties in your joint venture, the greater your chance of success. Not only will your teams have a personal investment in what the business is doing, but you will be able to draw on wider perceptions to further clarify your direction and improve the health of your business.

Make no mistake, there will be times when your team members won't all be on the same page. Your job as

---

5   The High Performance, 'Toto Wolff: Empathy over engineering; (Apple Podcasts), https://podcasts.apple.com/gb/podcast/toto-wolff-empathy-over-engineering/id1500444735?i=1000515748671

a leader is to listen to everyone and find a consensus. In those situations, you have to be brave and bold enough to make a strategic decision. Your team will need to be 100% behind you, regardless of whether they agree with your decision. Their total faith in your leadership and your ownership of your decisions will be the key to your overall success.

Remember that other people aren't aware of what's going on in your head. If your team members don't know what you have in mind and where you're going, it's unlikely you'll get there. The simplest way to counteract this is to have a morning huddle with your team: get everyone together with a cup of coffee to review what is coming up in the day ahead. Who is coming in? What are the priorities for the day? Are there any particular issues you all need to be aware of? Is anyone implementing anything new today?

This is how you set the direction for the team on a practical daily basis, and it complements the more formal meetings you have at monthly, quarterly and yearly intervals to review progress against your annual plan. At these meetings, you will be looking at targets. Your team members need to be well aware of what's expected of them in terms of, say, leads, conversions, treatments, patient satisfaction and the revenue collected.

On the money

Are you in control of your finances? No one wants to appear as if all they are interested in is money, but this really is a key question. If you don't have your finger on the pulse of your finances, you won't know where your business is going, and ultimately you won't be able to support your teams or your family. Neither will you be able to provide a reliable service to your patients. If you feel that you yourself are not good at keeping tabs on the money, employ someone to do it for you.

I have a bookkeeper who prepares monthly profit and loss accounts for all of my businesses, so I always have a clear picture of their position. If the figures fluctuate a little from month to month, that's fine, but if they're fluctuating a lot, I need to understand why it's happening and make course corrections with my teams as we go along.

In terms of financial planning and management, I have certain tried-and-tested parameters that I keep to as far as possible. For example, my marketing budget should be 2.5–5% of my total revenue and staff costs should be around 15%.

The way I see money in a business context is that it's like the fuel in a car. You can have the most amazing high-tech model of car, but it won't be going anywhere without fuel. You need to be shrewd and understand your numbers inside out, or if this isn't your forte, find a team member whose strength it is.

Free

This might seem a strange section to include in a level-headed practical book about the dental business, but in my view, freedom is a vital commodity. It's closely linked to the concept of self-actualisation that we find at the top of Maslow's hierarchy of needs.[6]

I first heard about Maslow's hierarchy of needs some years ago and his thinking really resonated with me. In analysing human motivation, he identified a scale of needs starting with physiological and moving up through safety, belonging and love, and esteem, before reaching the top of the hierarchy. Each stage must be satisfied within the individual themselves before they can be motivated by the next stage, with the ultimate goal being self-actualisation.

A vital part of self-actualisation is the freedom to choose what to do and how to spend your time. The aim is to reach a position where you can choose to do what really excites you. Consider whether you would get up and go in to work today even if nobody was going to pay you to do so. Ideally, you would want

---

6   AH Maslow, *A Theory Of Human Motivation* (Wilder Publications, 2018)

to, such is your engagement with the practice. By the same token, should the fancy take you to go to the beach instead, that would also be a possibility – if you've set up your business effectively.

If your mission is one you love, you will find it easy to be absorbed in the activities that running it entails. The beauty of reaching the 'freedom' status is that it will be up to you to decide whether this is a day when you will immerse yourself in the figures, achieving a state of flow through close analysis, or whether it's a day for some creative thinking about your latest social media campaign.

My exclusive focus on Invisalign offers me exactly that freedom of choice, and it's a sentiment I hear echoed by many other dentists I come across. All I can say is that for me, Invisalign has opened up the path to self-actualisation in a way I could not have imagined.

This brings us to the end of Part One, in which I've set out the MIWAY approach and how it has worked for me. We've touched on many of the practicalities of running a dental business along the way, but in Part Two, I want to look in detail at the options and requirements for you in building a dental business based on Invisalign.

PART TWO
WHAT YOU NEED TO DO

8
Marketing And Lead Generation

Customers are the lifeblood of any business, and dentistry is no exception. If you are going to adopt Invisalign in your practice and commit time and resources to doing so, you'll need a steady supply of patients to make it worth your while.

Before you launch a drive to promote Invisalign and sign people up for it, you need to ask yourself whether your practice is ready to receive new leads and follow them up. Is your team geared up to provide the level and quality of service that you need to offer as an Invisalign provider? You certainly don't want to be investing a penny in external marketing until you have agreed the processes and procedures you'll need to deal with new patients within your practice.

In this chapter, we'll explore the ins and outs of modern digital marketing, but believe me, the best place to start looking for patients is in your own practice.

Internal marketing

The inside-out approach

It's not always about going outside your business to find patients; your own clinic is a hotbed of potential. What's more, acquiring new customers for Invisalign from your existing patient base will cost you next to nothing.

First and foremost, you need to make patients aware that Invisalign is on offer at your practice. Invisalign itself will provide you with marketing materials such as banners and posters, and printed material that patients can take away with them, but perhaps the most important thing that you and your colleagues can do is to start a conversation with them – hence my focus on communication skills in my teams.

You literally have a captive audience: your patients. They are already aware of the quality of your work and quite comfortable with entrusting themselves to

Inside-out marketing

your care. Hopefully, your practice will feel like a safe and familiar place to them.

I'm not advocating a hard sell; it's more a question of drawing to the attention of those you think might be interested in the treatment the fact that it's available. You will know from your contact with patients who has expressed concern about the look of their teeth or those for whom misaligned teeth are causing other problems.

I would also suggest using your iTero scanner on every patient. It makes it a lot easier to initiate that conversation about whether they have ever considered having their teeth straightened if they can actually see what you are talking about. In the end, all you are doing is setting out your stall; the rest is up to them.

Open days

Whether you're just starting out with Invisalign or have an established practice, open days are a good way of reaching new patients. They offer a completely risk-free no-pressure opportunity for potential patients to come to your dental practice and meet your team. The visitors can spend time with you and get all their questions answered, free from the constraints of an ordinary appointment.

Open days are useful for your existing patients as well as people new to your practice precisely because they offer contact in a relaxed and unpressured context. It's best to keep the day free of normal appointments, so that all the premises are available to view and members of the team are free to chat to your visitors. I'd recommend running open days once a quarter.

Once you've fixed a date for an open day, you need to text or email all your patients to encourage them to come along, as well as advertising it on social media. Visitors will expect to meet and greet the team, and to get lots of useful information along the way, but if you can offer them something more, so much the better. Most practices will include a free scan, teeth whitening or retention for those who sign up at an open day.

External marketing

Lead generation is all about finding the patients that are as yet unknown to you, but are the right fit for your business. Delivering the right message to the right person at the right time is the key to successful marketing. By way of general context, Align invests heavily in promotional campaigns to increase Invisalign brand awareness in the UK, so you can capitalise on the relatively high profile it has.

In the context of your aspirations for your own practice, you need as comprehensive a picture as possible of your potential patients: where they live, what they do, what media they consume and what they aspire to. The answers to all these questions lie in the vast amounts of data that are now available.

At MiSmile, we work with agency experts since they are experienced in mining and analysing all this data. This gives us insights into where to find our patients. Agency experts are also experienced in keeping up with any new channels that are gaining in popularity and understanding their demographic. Together, we devise a strategy for how best to reach out to the people who are likely to have an interest in Invisalign.

One of my key messages throughout this book is to recognise that you are the expert in treating patients, so work with others who can do the bits that you are not expert at. While you may not necessarily need to go and find an agency, you definitely need to make good use of your time by focusing on what you're good at and partnering with people who are experts in fields you're not so good at.

I'd recommend you partner with an agency or an individual you feel you 'gel' with. Ask to see evidence of their track record and speak to their other customers before you enter into any kind of commitment. The right agency or marketing expert will be able to advise you on your overall strategy, create a compelling web presence for you, and be open about their results and their ongoing plans.

Dentists who join the MiSmile Network will have access to a central agency. This will manage their lead generation for them, but I would always recommend finding out as much as you can about other marketing agencies and what they have to offer. It's part of educating yourself to have the knowledge you need to ask the right questions if you work with an agency in the future.

Social media and digital channels

Someone recently commented to me that consumers don't so much go online any more as live online. For this reason, social media has become the forum in which to find the right customers for your business, but you need to know who is using it and how.

Instagram is the platform of choice for the classic Invisalign patient, the twenty-five to thirty-five-year-old female, whereas TikTok and Snapchat are used more by younger people. Popular though it is, Facebook is now primarily the domain of older Invisalign patients.

Bear in mind that the quality of the leads generated by these different platforms varies and take this into consideration when considering digital advertising. If I have £10,000 to spend on marketing, I will probably put 95% of it into digital advertisements, but within this category, I have a choice between Google and social media channels.

Anyone actively looking for dental alignment treatment is likely to type 'invisible braces' or something similar into the Google search engine, so you know that when they see your advertisement, it will be the answer to their question. On social media channels, your advertisement is scrolling past someone who fits the demographic for your business, but who is not necessarily looking for dental alignment at the moment. The leads generated by Google are, therefore, likely to be far quicker to convert than those arising from social media.

Your website

The initial advertising is only part of the process of recruiting new patients. Where are you going to send them once they have clicked on your advertisement or seen some information about you? At MiSmile, we have both a website and a landing page, and they play different roles. The website is informative and generic, providing an overview of who we are and what we do at MiSmile, whereas the landing page, while still providing that information, is more targeted, more of a call to action.

What the landing page enables my teams and I to do is capture leads' data. We ask for the potential patient's email address and/or their phone number. Once we have that data, we can begin to nurture a relationship with them.

A key point to note is that most of your potential audience will be looking at your website or your landing page on a mobile phone, so you need to make sure that both are mobile optimised and ready to receive traffic from mobiles. Although they're quite small, these pages need to look good, and be clear and concise. You don't necessarily need a web designer as there are lots of free templates online to help you create them, but remember, you are probably not an expert in this field. Professional design doesn't cost a fortune.

Lead conversion

What you do with the lead information, whether it be an email address or a phone number, is the key to growth. I realised the importance of follow up early on in my Invisalign career when I was investing more and more into lead generation and dealing with an increasing number of Invisalign cases. For a while, my practice manager, my receptionist, my dental nurse and I all tried to follow up the leads as well as we could, but I didn't feel we were giving each prospect enough focus.

That's when I did some research and found out about a fairly new role in many dental practices: the TCO. It was a bit of a leap of faith, but I employed one in my own practice and have never looked back.

CASE STUDY: A DAY IN THE LIFE OF A TCO

Parmjit Kaur, the TCO at MiSmile Birmingham, tells us what a typical day looks like in her role.

'When I come in, I have a morning coffee in the team huddle while we set our goals for the day, so we are all on the same page. Then I have a one-to-one catch up with the marketing manager to see how many leads we had the day before and what the quality of the leads is like.

'I go through the dentists' diaries to see which new patients are coming in. This means I can give each dentist a little debrief, so they have some background about the patient before they walk in. I always write notes against the appointments anyway, just in case they forget.

'I set aside a thirty-minute admin period before I see my patients, so I can reply to emails. After that, consultations start. These consist of greeting the patient, perhaps talking about their day to put them at their ease, explaining Invisalign, doing a scan, going through the finance options and booking them in for treatment.

'At midday, I like to have another little catch up with the team to see how everyone is doing. The afternoon is taken up with consultations. I usually send each patient a personalised treatment plan after their visit, but if my appointments are back to back, I'll do these at the end of the day.'

The TCO has become a pivotal role in my team structure. We have really seen the benefits at MiSmile of having a dedicated member of the team responsible for following up leads once people have made an enquiry, booking them in for a consultation, and then leading that consultation.

Customer relationship management (CRM)

Brilliant as the TCO is, she could not keep up with the volume of enquiries coming in as we did more and more marketing, so I made the big decision to invest in a CRM system. It was a big decision as mine was one of the first dental practices to use such a system. What really appealed to me about it was its capacity to send 'nurture' emails to prospects once they had made an enquiry; this made a big impact on MiSmile's ability to get patients booked in.

Fast forward a few years, and at MiSmile we now use DenGro, which has been built specifically for the dental industry. It both registers and maintains contact with the potential patient or lead ('keeping it warm', as the saying goes), and it generates a dashboard of tasks for the practice team, so that we know a new lead has come in and we've got to follow it up. We know that the chances of converting a lead into a new patient are significantly higher if we contact them within two hours of their enquiry.

This system has been invaluable for everyone in the MiSmile Network. It's enabled us to get the right balance between overdoing the contact with patients and ignoring them completely. Once a patient has made an initial enquiry with us, we follow a step-by-step guide as to how we approach them after that and through which channels.

DenGro has significantly increased our conversion rate at MiSmile. The data we extract from it is invaluable in planning our future marketing activity as we know exactly who has converted and where they heard about us.

Timing is everything

People buy when the time is right for them, which partly explains why Google advertising is often more fruitful than social media advertising. On Google, you're addressing the people who have, for the most part, decided that the time is now.

As for the rest, they may be the perfect customers to benefit from Invisalign treatment, but they are not yet ready. Part of being realistic about the occasional frustrations of running a business is accepting that. There will come a time when they perhaps overhear a remark about someone else's teeth or have an important event coming up such as a wedding, and they will take the decision to proceed. That's when you want to be the organisation they reach out to.

Invisalign is a high-value item and as with any high-value item – a car, a sofa, a holiday – people will shop around. If you don't get back to a lead in a timely fashion, they'll forget all about you and go on to someone else instead. Careful timing of messages through appropriate platforms is something that your patients will really value.

Checklist

I can't emphasise enough that how you follow up on leads matters. You might have invested time, money and a lot of effort into finding new patients, but if your team isn't geared up to follow enquiries through, you might as well be throwing money down the drain. Make sure you've got your internal processes right and your teams know how to follow up these leads before you start spending large sums on external marketing.

As we're now getting into the practicalities of running your business, I am going to be including a handy checklist at the end of every chapter in this part. Here's a recap of how to go about marketing your practice successfully and converting the interested enquiries into patients:

- Make sure your team members are signed up to and prepared for an increase in patient numbers from your planned marketing activity.

- Your present practice probably contains potential Invisalign patients – do they know you offer it?

- Do your research before partnering up with a marketing agency.

- If you don't have one already, consider employing a TCO to handle all new patient enquiries.

- Ensure you have a CRM system like DenGro that can keep your leads warm and communicate with them in a timely fashion.

- Use the data in your CRM system to identify where your patients are coming from and inform your future marketing plans.

9
Shaping The Patient Journey

Even the quickest and most straightforward of dental procedures involves a leap of faith on the part of the patient. They are literally opening themselves up to a virtual stranger and allowing them to wield sharp instruments inside their mouth – no wonder some people get nervous.

This is why, if I had only £10,000 to invest in my business, I would spend it on people first, then technology, and finally on external marketing. I get the best return on investment through having people in my practice who will build trust with the patients, meaning they can embark on their journey with confidence.

Your team

Just as your practice is likely to be a fruitful source of Invisalign patients, I would advise you to look there for possible candidates before recruiting for your expanding team. Your dental nurse, for example, may be the perfect person to take on a new role as a TCO.

The more important the role is to the business, the more reluctant I am to go out and hire people I don't know. I have a strong relationship with everyone in my existing team, so it's my responsibility to understand their strengths and weaknesses, and how the dynamics of the team work.

Anyone in the practice who expresses an interest in moving into a new role will get support for doing this. Through shadowing someone in the role or taking formal courses where appropriate, they will get every opportunity to develop the necessary skills to make a move. I might not be able to make it happen for them within the first year or two, but we'll work to an agreed timescale.

I want my people to be able to see the future. Do they know that if they help the business reach its targets, they will share in that success? Do they know what the next step for them looks like? Put yourself in your team members' shoes. Yes, they will help you to get to where you want to be, but will you help them get where they want to go?

Quite apart from the effectiveness of a motivated, close-knit team – and the pleasure to be had from working with such a team – do not underestimate the advantages it brings in terms of staff retention. The average cost of recruiting a new member of staff is estimated to be £3,000,[7] so the savings from not having to do so are obvious.

People tend to think that retaining staff is all about money, but it's not. Of course, it's important to pay your team a fair salary, but what really keeps them in your practice is the satisfaction they derive from their work. If the members of your team enjoy their work, it will enhance the experience patients have at your practice.

Training

I make time for monthly and quarterly reviews with all my team members. I need to know what gets them out of bed in the morning and where their ambitions lie, so I make a point of asking them a classic question:

'Where do you see yourself in five years' time?'

Everybody in my practice, no matter what their role, will have a training plan. The training offered by Invisalign is a must for qualified dentists actually administering the treatment, but the ongoing professional

---

7   Glassdoor Team, 'How to calculate your cost-per-hire' (Glassdoor for Employers, 2020), www.glassdoor.co.uk/employers/blog/calculate-cost-per-hire

development of their colleagues in the practice is no less important. There are plenty of courses and other opportunities to develop further skills among your team, be they business, communication or marketing skills, or anything else that would serve the needs of both the practice and the individual.

Mentoring and coaching are also hugely important. Regard yourself as the coach for your team, encouraging their development and enhancing their contribution to the practice. You don't necessarily have to sign up to every idea they put forward, but they need to feel engaged with the direction the practice is heading in and confident that they have a voice in it.

Communication skills training is vital for all team members who deal with patients. Every touch point with the patient shapes their journey, so are your team members trained to support your patients and be advocates of the practice? If any member of the team doesn't buy into this approach, patients will notice and it can undermine the great work you do.

Delegating

I know that people sometimes struggle to delegate, but I can't say it's something that I've ever had a problem with. I believe in delegating wherever possible. My only proviso is that the person you are delegating to must be absolutely clear about what you are asking them to do and the outcome that you expect. That's all. Don't teach them how to do it; just let them find their own way within an agreed timescale. Do be available, though, for whenever they need to come to you with a query or for advice.

If you hover over them, micromanaging and monitoring their every move, not only will it sap their confidence, it will fritter away the time you ought to have been saving by delegating.

Managing performance

With well-motivated staff being given all the support we've just looked at, dealing with poor performance won't be something you have to do often. If you do see evidence of it – if someone has failed to deliver on what was agreed – take rapid action rather than just hoping the problem will go away.

This action needs to take the form of an in-depth conversation with your team member to understand exactly why they have missed their targets. Sometimes it may be because of factors beyond their control, so you need to address whatever the problem is, but if it happens quarter after quarter, despite reviews and agreement on achievable targets, you may need to make the difficult decision that the person in question is simply not suitable for the job in hand. If you start accepting mediocre results, you'll end up with a mediocre team.

Patient-facing roles

It's essential for the quality of the patient journey that team members' roles are clearly delineated and they know exactly what they are meant to be doing, and when. The patient should never feel as though they don't know what's going to happen next or that they don't have any choice, or worry about how much money they are going to have to spend.

We touched on the patient-facing roles earlier in the book; now let's look at them in more detail.

New patient coordinator (NPC)

When someone gets in touch for the first time – a new lead who has contacted your practice by phone, email or through your website, or been referred by an existing patient – the NPC kicks their journey off. The role of the NPC is to build rapport with the patient, give them all the information they need about the clinic and encourage them to take the next step of booking an appointment with the TCO.

When a patient has reached out, it's the job of a dental practice team to understand what their trigger point has been. What is the emotion behind their wish to improve their smile? Are they embarrassed about their teeth, perhaps? Or do they just want to look their best for a big day? When the NPC is talking to a patient, they will be making a note of all these things, so that when the patient is handed on to the TCO, this information goes too.

Front of house

First impressions are vitally important, so the person who welcomes new patients into your practice has a huge responsibility. This may be a receptionist or a concierge, but the aim is the same: to make sure the patient is comfortable, help them to complete any paperwork that is necessary, and answer any initial queries before passing them on to the TCO.

Treatment coordinator (TCO)

The information they receive from the NPC gives the TCO the opportunity to get the conversation with the patient off to a flying start. They'll be able to congratulate the patient on her upcoming wedding and ask her if she's chosen her dress, for example. The TCO could even invite her to think about how wonderful it will be to look back on her dazzling smile in her wedding photos twenty years from now.

The TCO is in effect acting as a consultant, in the literal sense of the word. Their job is to add value by listening to the patient carefully (possibly even picking up on some of what is not being said), questioning them to gain clarification and identifying what their needs are. Then they set out the best possible options for the patient's treatment, what each option will cost and arrangements for payment, to let the patient decide what works best for them.

TCOs are often responsible for generating revenue, so they will also be monitoring the marketing spend, how many leads it is generating, how many of them are coming in for consultations and how many are actually proceeding to treatment. Once the patient has taken that final step, they are handed over to the clinical team.

The clinical team

The patient is now in the hands of the dentist and the dental nurse for treatment. You will know from your professional experience the qualities that you look for in good dental staff.

Technically, of course, as dentists, we straighten, fill, scale and polish people's teeth, but ultimately what we do is change their lives. We're in the business of giving people amazing smiles, leading to improved confidence so they can go out and get what they want from life.

If your clinical team members feel that this is what they are working for, that will communicate itself to the patients, who in turn will feel respected and valued. Hundreds of clinics offer teeth straightening; the USP lies in meeting patients' emotional needs.

Patient reassurance

Making the most of technology

You could describe to your patient the finer points of the dental alignment you are about to undertake with them and the results you expect from it – or you could just show them a picture. A picture, as the saying goes, is worth a thousand words.

Integrate technology at every stage of the patient's treatment. 'SmileView' technology means that you can take a photo of the patient and within sixty seconds show them what their smile will look like. The iTero scanner is more than just a clinical tool for producing the scans from which the aligners will be made; it can give your patient instant 'before' and 'after' views. At the beginning of the chapter, I described dentistry as feeling like a leap of faith for patients, but this technology removes the need for faith. What they see is exactly what they will be getting.

Affordability

Dental alignment is a big-ticket item, so the patient's sense that this is a huge financial commitment is often at war with their desire to improve their smile.

This is why one of my team's questions for patients when they come to the MiSmile clinic is about how they would like to pay for the treatment. We aim to make the treatment as affordable as possible and offer patients a number of different arrangements to suit all scenarios:

- If they have the funds available, they can pay up front at the beginning of treatment, and they'll receive a small discount to reflect the admin costs that this will save the business.

- We can offer them interest-free finance over twelve months.

- We can extend finance over a period of five years at a reasonable rate of interest, which could bring the cost of treatment down to as little as £30 a month.

- Patients also have the option to pay as they go, putting in half the total cost up front and paying off the rest throughout the course of their treatment, over the next six to twelve months.

What's important for them to remember is that teeth alignment is not vanity; it's an investment in themselves and their confidence to go out and take on the world.

Aftercare

Our dentition is a complex system. While undergoing Invisalign treatment, patients need to maintain the position of their teeth. They do this by means of retainers, which can be fixed or removable. Fixed retainers are glued to the back of the teeth, whereas removable retainers are worn only at night.

At MiSmile, we take a belt-and-braces approach (no pun intended) to make sure the teeth never move. We provide fixed retainers, supplemented by removable Vivera retainers made by Align Technology. Once all the treatment is finished, patients leave the clinic with a clear understanding of how to maintain their smile, written aftercare advice showing them how to use their removable retainers and look after their teeth.

Pride yourself on having a long-term relationship with your patients. The starting point for that can be a guarantee on all your work – at MiSmile, we offer a twelve-month guarantee. If the teeth continue to move after the treatment has finished or if something breaks or if anything is not the way the patient would like it to be, while the work is still under guarantee, the practice will fix it free of charge.

You could also encourage patients to join a membership plan. For a small monthly fee, they get a routine six-monthly check-up, hygiene appointments and a discount on further treatments, such as whitening.

Complaints

When you're running a business, no matter how effective your operation, you will never be able to avoid complaints completely. There will always be someone whose expectations you have failed to meet.

Funny though it sounds, I love the complainers because they give me a real opportunity to learn. What I don't want is somebody who is not 100% happy with their treatment walking away at the end of it without telling my team what they didn't like.

Dissatisfied patients give you the opportunity to put things right. If you put things right for them immediately without fuss, they will become your patients for life. Whatever it is – something to do with waiting times or the availability of appointments, or even the end result – understand what went wrong, make good with the patient and amend your operating procedures or your clinical practice if necessary.

CASE STUDY: ENHANCING THE PATIENT EXPERIENCE

At MiSmile here in Birmingham, our patient journey has evolved over many years and, for now at least, we have a seamless patient experience that has without a doubt helped with patient conversion.

We provide a clear online booking function on the website and landing pages. When an appointment request comes in, we strive to call the patient back within two hours to confirm their appointment with the TCO.

Patients are greeted at the door by our receptionist and taken to our Invisalign SmileView area. While there, they can take a selfie and see what their new smile could look like, all in just 60 seconds. This provides the 'wow' factor and excites them for the next step in their journey.

The TCO will then scan them using the iTero scanner and talk through treatments in more detail. If they're keen to proceed, a second appointment is booked by the dentist and a deposit taken.

We're always looking for ways to improve this patient journey and use checks and balances during monthly team meetings. The most important aspect is that the patient is the focal point of everything we do.

Checklist

A seamless journey from first contact to leaving your clinic with a dazzling confident smile is what your patients have a right to expect. Here's a checklist for the steps we've covered in this chapter that are essential for ensuring you can provide that journey:

- Build a strong, motivated team through regular feedback, targeted training and offering opportunities for progression in your practice.

- Act as coach and mentor to your colleagues, and invite their participation in the development of the practice.

- Ensure you delegate effectively, so colleagues acquire the skills they need to progress.

- Keep on top of performance management to maintain the quality of the service you are offering.

- Ensure you have the appropriate staff filling the key posts in your practice and that they understand the part they have to play in a successful patient journey.

- Remember that patients' emotional needs are as important as their clinical needs.

- Maintain the relationship with your patients by providing an attractive aftercare plan.

10
Clinical Confidence

You have the MIWAY framework from Part One, but what about the actual service you'll be offering? How can you be sure that Invisalign is the best product and the most effective process for your patients?

One powerful way to create a strong, reliable brand for your practice and amplify your credibility is to leverage the reputation of key suppliers, like Align Technology and its Invisalign brand. Let's explore Invisalign and the company behind it, so you can be assured that in growing your practice based on Invisalign, you'll be supported all the way by a company whose technology and methods have a proven record of success.

Align Technology

Align Technology with its global headquarters in Arizona, US was founded in 1997 by Zia Chishti and Kelsey Wirth, and since then, ten million people have been treated with the Invisalign system. At first it was used exclusively by orthodontists, but in 2001, it became available for use by general dentists.

Zia Chishti's initial idea came to him when he was an adult orthodontic patient. He realised that you could use soft plastic aligners rather than rigid retainers and thereby effect large movements in dentition in incremental stages. Since its launch, Align Technology has become worth $2bn and operates in three regions: the Americas, Asia Pacific, and Europe, the Middle East and Africa (EMEA). Its EMEA headquarters are in Switzerland.

In a period of just two years, between 2002 and 2004, Invisalign grew from 80,000 patients to 175,000. The system won several awards for stereolithography (a form of 3D printing technology) and medical design. If that doesn't convince you of its reputability, I don't know what will!

Invisalign

Invisalign has a number of products on offer: Invisalign Comprehensive, Invisalign Lite, Invisalign

Express, Invisalign Go and Invisalign Go Plus. Invisalign Go and Invisalign Go Plus are designed specifically for non-specialists.

The MiSmile Network focuses on Invisalign Comprehensive, Invisalign Lite, Invisalign Go and Go Plus. I encourage members to leave the more complex cases to the specialists. The beauty of Invisalign Go is that it's simple and the initial training will give you everything you need to get started.

Invisalign training

The basic Invisalign training is a three-day course, run over six months, which can be taken online or in person.

- **Day one** covers the theory, ensuring that you have an understanding of the basic principles behind clear aligners.

- **Day two** is the practical training, including the use of the iTero scanner and covering everything from dental techniques like interproximal reduction (creating small amounts of space between pairs of teeth to allow them to move) to setting up treatment plans correctly and monitoring the progress of your cases.

- **Day three** brings together everything you've learned on the previous two days by addressing all the questions and concerns that may have arisen during the training. At this stage, you are encouraged to bring your own cases for discussion and initial guidance on how to handle them.

By the end of the training, you should have the confidence to go out and treat simple cases. As the number and variety of cases you treat grow, so will your experience and expertise, supplemented by the ongoing training and development offered by the Invisalign team.

Invisalign technology

The technology behind Invisalign makes it easy for dentists to get consistently good results. The company's artificial intelligence-driven platform enables dentists to upload their prospective cases and receive guidance on the complete set of photos they will need to supply for the manufacture of the aligners. This guidance is based on the machine learning drawn from the millions of Invisalign cases completed to date.

Once your case is uploaded, the Invisalign system guides you through the treatment by means of a traffic light system. If your proposed course of action is absolutely right, you get the green light, but if there is a particular issue you need to be aware of, you will get an amber alert. A red light will warn you of potential mistakes. This gives you the reassurance that you will not be able to undertake any action that could be detrimental to your patient, and that any cases you need to refer to an orthodontist will be flagged up. This continuous oversight of your cases means that you can proceed with confidence, secure in the knowledge that Invisalign has you covered.

General support

Align Technology invests heavily in brand awareness and marketing, educating the consumer about clear aligners, Invisalign's pre-eminence in this field, and the relative ease of getting a nice straight smile. This publicity forms the backdrop to all of your own marketing efforts, ensuring that many prospective patients have already gained knowledge of what can be achieved and are motivated to seek treatment. Align Technology also provides a dentist locator, where people can enter their postcode and find out about all the providers in their area, with details of their experience and full range of services.

Align Technology's administrative structure includes sales teams and territory managers. Territory managers are your first port of call for any queries: how to plan a treatment and set it up correctly on the system; queries about Invisalign innovations; and so on. They will be able to help you with most issues, and if there is anything they can't handle, they will find the person you need to speak to.

Complementary procedures

The popularity of the 'align, bleach and bond' package has never been higher. The reason dentists and patients love it is because together, the three techniques constitute a minimally invasive treatment with maximum impact. Straightening, whitening and a bit of bonding can give anyone the perfect smile.

Both the manufacturers of the products in question and dentists who have extensive experience in these procedures offer training in these techniques.

Bleaching

If people have spent nine to twelve months getting their teeth straightened, they are likely to want to show this off with a nice, bright smile. The old days of the preferred treatment being porcelain veneers, which entailed grinding down perfectly healthy teeth, are long gone. The most convenient method is home whitening, making use of the Invisalign clear plastic aligners that the patients will already have from the final stage of their treatment. The dentist then provides the patient with the gel and comprehensive instructions explaining what they have to do.

There are various types of whitening gels on the market, but the one we use at MiSmile is Enlighten. Patients have a choice of Day White or Night White. The Day White preparation entails the patient wearing their gel-filled tray for two hours during the day; the Night White one is used overnight, while the patient sleeps.

Teeth whitening is now being offered in hair salons and beauty clinics, but in my opinion, this is risky. Ideally, this treatment needs to be done under the supervision of a qualified dentist, and it's worth bearing in mind that it's not recommended for those under eighteen and pregnant women.

Patients also need to be aware that the results are not permanent, and that how long the improvement lasts will depend on their diet. Tea, coffee, red wine and curry will all darken the teeth again, and fizzy drinks don't help, either.

Bonding

Bonding is a technique used to build up a tooth if the patient has chipped it or if it is smaller than the neighbouring teeth. Again, it avoids the need for grinding down teeth that crowns and veneers entail. Someone who has been through the straightening process need not worry that their smile will be undermined by a chipped tooth or one that, however well aligned, is not the same size as the rest.

If bonding is skilfully executed, no one will be able to tell where the composite ends and the original tooth enamel begins. The learning curve is perhaps steeper than with Invisalign itself, but it's a reversible procedure and patients love it.

With proper care, bonding will last for ten to fifteen years. It might need fully replacing or touching up after that.

Who is Invisalign for?

In the chapter on marketing, we discussed the types of people who are most likely to be interested in Invisalign, but from a clinical point of view, nearly anyone is a suitable candidate for it. An experienced Invisalign dentist can treat 95% of the cases that come before them. Only in a small number of these cases will the work needed be so complex that alignment has to be achieved through the traditional approach, involving fixed metal braces composed of brackets and wires. These cases need to be referred to a specialist orthodontist, in line with the Invisalign advice.

We don't administer Invisalign for teenagers at MiSmile, so our youngest patient was sixteen years old. Children have to have lost all their milk teeth and acquired their adult dentition before receiving Invisalign treatment, so patients are unlikely to be younger than ten years old.

CASE STUDY: YOU'RE NEVER TOO OLD FOR THE PERFECT SMILE

Our oldest patient at MiSmile was a sixty-seven-year-old woman – let's call her Sylvie. All her life, she had shied away from having her teeth aligned; the idea of a mouth full of metal was just too much for her to bear, so she hid the gap in her teeth behind a closed-lipped smile.

It was a chance conversation with a MiSmile patient, after Sylvie had admired this person's bright white smile, that convinced her that the boat hadn't actually sailed when it came to getting her teeth fixed. It took her a few weeks to pluck up the courage to get in touch, but once she had made that initial contact, the smoothness of the customer journey made the procedure a breeze from then on. Less than a year later, Sylvie is delighted with her results. Gone is the closed-lipped smile; now she beams radiantly at every opportunity.

Invisalign is a treatment with near-enough universal applicability, so there is no reason for anyone to feel as though they have missed the boat when it comes to improving their smile.

Checklist

Launching or expanding your Invisalign practice is a big step. These are the factors that will justify your decision to proceed:

- Align Technology is a global company with an estimated yearly revenue of over $2bn whose products are endorsed at the highest level.

- The Invisalign method is simple to learn, after which you can expand your expertise at your own pace.

- Align Technology provides comprehensive support for dentists, including territory managers to help you with any issues that arise.

- Align Technology continuously promotes consumer awareness of the Invisalign brand.

- Bleaching and bonding are services that are often added to alignment to form a comprehensive package for patients.

- Basic Invisalign treatment is suitable for 95% of your patients.

11
Building A Profitable Business

So much depends on what your ambitions are. If your current business is working well, then it's definitely worth considering whether to expand your clinic and start offering other services. Also, don't forget yourself – personal development is vitally important so that you can learn new skills and offer them to your patients.

You need to have a clear idea, based on the real-world experience of practices similar to yours, how likely, and how quickly, you can expect to recoup any investment you have made.

Investment

If you are looking to set up your first practice, you may have to be creative in putting together the funding to achieve this. Perhaps you could beg or borrow – but not steal – from friends and family, or withdraw some funds from the bank of Mum and Dad.

Once you have been going for a couple of years and have proof of a steady track record over this period, you should be able to get a bank loan. If you go to the business adviser in your local bank with evidence of what you have already achieved and a sound plan for what you are prepared to achieve in the future, they are often willing to invest in dentistry. Dentistry, for them, is something of a safe bet, so many financiers are falling over each other to put their money into it.

In view of this, as well as the number of dentists leaving the profession, there's probably never been a better time to set up or expand your own practice.

Return on investment

There is a rough equation between every £1,000 invested and the number of people going ahead with treatment that reflects a process of attrition as you go from one stage to the next:

- For every £1,000 you invest on digital marketing, you can expect twenty to thirty people to make an enquiry with you, so let's assume you invest £3,000 and get 100 enquiries.

- You can expect sixty of them (ie 60%) to come in for a consultation.

- Of these, forty will go ahead with an oral health assessment.

- Thirty of these forty prospects will be suitable for treatment and take it up.

DenGro is the perfect platform to help you understand your return on investment. It can give you an end-to-end picture of how your funnel is working and flag up for you when additional action is needed. The minimum return I'm generally prepared to accept is 10%, so in our example above, I will expect to make at least £30,000 out of my initial outlay of £3,000. When you're working hard at full capacity, that return can obviously be far greater.

Naturally, you need to be reinvesting some of that profit into the business, and you will know the areas that need expenditure, whether it's upgrading equipment or refurbishing premises. As a fairly reliable rule of thumb, I would recommend investing 2.5–5% of your revenue into marketing.

If you find that your returns are inadequate, you need to undertake some rigorous analysis of where things are going wrong. This may lead to some tough decisions, especially if the cause is underperforming staff. If something isn't working, don't just ignore it and hope it will get better; you need to face it.

Contingency plans

There's no escaping the fact that sometimes things go wrong or the unexpected happens – the Covid pandemic has taught us all that. What do you need to do to be prepared for a rainy day?

My rule of thumb is to have enough funds in your account to cover you for at least three months. Even if you didn't earn anything at all during this time, you would still be able to pay your staff and your suppliers, and cover rental costs. This is something I have always been mindful of, and it meant that when the pandemic hit in 2020, I could be fairly relaxed about it. Of course, if you can extend your contingency fund to cover your business for six months, then so much the better.

Defaults

The next section deals with arrangements for offering patients credit. It's quite rare for them to default on their payments, but you still have to take into account the possibility that it will happen as part of your business plan.

It's wise to assume that an amount representing 0.5% of your turnover will be lost to bad debt. This means that on a turnover of £1m, you will have to write off £5,000. If you're prepared for it, you will be able to respond calmly as and when it happens.

Insurance

Of course, no dentist is allowed to practise without indemnity insurance, but there is additional insurance available from specialist companies if you are undertaking an extremely complex treatment such as implants or complete mouth rehabilitation. I would certainly advise taking out this type of insurance in such cases.

Patient finance

Even though Invisalign has brought dental alignment within the financial reach of many more people than before, it's still a big commitment for patients. At MiSmile, we are keen to make it affordable to as many people as possible, so we offer patients who would prefer not to pay the whole amount upfront two types of credit.

One point to note is that if you are offering either interest-free or charged-for credit, you will need approval from the Financial Conduct Authority (FCA). The FCA will want to be confident that you will treat patients making use of your credit honestly and fairly.

Interest-free credit

With MiSmile, patients can take an interest-free loan over twelve months. If, for example, their treatment is to cost £3,000 overall, they will pay MiSmile £250 a month for a year. My team and I work with a finance company that pays us the whole amount at the start of the treatment, but takes 6% to cover its costs. Yes, we lose that 6% on the cost of the treatment, but this arrangement is worthwhile for us in that it guarantees our cash flow.

If at any time patients find that they can't keep up with their payments, they can transfer to an arrangement that entails a lower monthly payment, but attracts interest. We are here to help our patients, and as long as they come to us with a reasonable request, we are happy to consider rescheduling their payments.

Paid-for credit

If patients want to pay for their treatment over a longer period than twelve months, there are different options for the amount of their monthly repayments. On average, they will be charged 9.9% in interest.

We at MiSmile do everything we can to make it as clear to patients as possible what they are committing themselves to using simple calculations. The TCO is happy to sit down with a patient and play around with different repayment options until they find a monthly rate that they are comfortable with.

Expansion

Chapter 8 deals in detail with marketing and how to increase your patient base, but I will take this opportunity to repeat that the best place to start looking for your Invisalign patients is among your existing patients. I have recommended setting aside 2.5–5% of your revenue for marketing, but don't spend any of it until you have ensured that everyone attending your practice is aware of all the services you have to offer. This is what I call the 'inside-out' approach.

One vital element of expanding into Invisalign is the purchase of the iTero scanner, but this is an investment that will pay for itself in five years. Bear in mind that the last thing you want with a big-ticket item like a scanner is for it to be lying idle, so I strongly recommend that you train up your staff to use the scanner in the way that is most appropriate for their role. The TCO needs to be able to use the scanner to generate 'before' and 'after' images as part of advising patients. Dental nurses need to be trained to do X-rays under your supervision, to use the iTero scanner and to take photos of the patient's dentition. One of the benefits of Invisalign is that the whole team can be involved in patient care, with the result that your time is freed up.

In a dental practice, the most valuable commodity is the dentist's time. The more you are able to delegate, the more cases you will be able to take on, ensuring growth in your skills, your team's skills and your patient cohort. Taking on complex cases is rewarding both intellectually and financially.

Enhancing your status

Invisalign has a scheme designed to encourage and support growth in your business by acknowledging your expertise through its graded provider status. It awards the dentist points on the basis of the different types of Invisalign treatment they have undertaken:

- Invisalign Comprehensive – 100 points

- Invisalign Lite – 60 points

- Vivera retainers – 10 points

Points are also awarded for training and education, so you benefit from continually developing your clinical experience.

The grading runs from Bronze to Diamond Two, depending on the number of points you have earned in a year. To sustain your status, you need to continue to treat the same number of cases year on year.

The scheme is an inclusive one, designed to nurture dentists to grow as gradually or as rapidly as they wish.

Aim to start with twenty cases in the first year and increase by twenty cases a year. That is achievable and sustainable, and in five years' time, you will be doing 100 cases a year. Go below this pace and it is harder to build your expertise, become familiar with a range of cases and gain experience of the more complex ones. This is another good reason for ensuring that your time is freed up as far as possible: it will allow for maximum exposure to challenging cases and plenty of time for drawing on the expertise of the dedicated Invisalign customer support team.

CASE STUDY: GROWTH FOR ALL

Dr Erika Schoeman of Elegance Dental talks about joining the MiSmile Network to enable her practice's growth.

'As I love providing Invisalign for my patients and seeing their joy at achieving the smile they always wanted, it was an easy decision for me to join the MiSmile Network. MiSmile has supported me continuously and I'm so proud of Elegance Dental's steady year-on-year growth pattern. The training and guidance, as well as advice on what to avoid, are invaluable, and the procedure and processes my team now have in place have resulted in a slick, professional patient journey.

'I'm delighted that we're now well on our way to achieving Diamond Status. Not only has every member of my team grown in capability and experience as our case volume has increased, they have also bought in to the overall vision of achieving this prestigious status. It really is a win-win for all of us.'

Checklist

Whether you are a bold entrepreneurial spirit or someone who may only recently have considered branching out into cosmetic dentistry, Invisalign offers a rewarding and reliable way for you to expand. There are some simple principles to keep in mind as you grow your business:

- You may need to be creative in finding initial sources of funding so that you can build a track record that will lead to eligibility for a bank loan.

- As a rough rule of thumb, every £1,000 of investment in marketing your practice will bring in ten new patients.

- Ensure you always have in your account enough funds to cover your costs for three months in case of an emergency – such as a pandemic.

- Be prepared to write off 0.5% of your revenue to bad debt.

- Flexible payment arrangements will make treatment more accessible for patients and ensure a smooth cash flow for your practice.

- Invisalign offers a comprehensive grading scheme to support you in developing your skills and expanding your practice.

Conclusion

One thing is for sure: when I was working as a dental nurse in an NHS practice back in 2000, if someone had come to me and said, 'One day you will become a dentist and you will own more than one dental practice', I would have told them to get real. Yet now, I'm running multiple dental practices, both NHS and private, and leading the MiSmile Network and Mastering your Invisalign Business programmes.

Sometimes I have to stop and figure out exactly how I got here. On reflection, it boils down to a couple of things. The first is my 'What's next?' attitude; throughout my professional life, this one question has always helped me to look forward and plan for the future. I also know I can't go it alone. I had to build a team around myself of people who get me, my mission, my goals and my values, and whose skills complement mine. Over the years, I have been blessed to find and retain an amazing group of colleagues who are my biggest assets.

Alongside this, maintaining an unwavering focus on one thing has been the key to my success. In this social-media-driven world, it's easy to be tempted by lots of shiny opportunities, but I set out to build my business around the Invisalign niche. Today I can tell you that this relentless focus has helped me to build a great business balanced with an amazing personal life.

There is no such thing as a typical day in my life. One day, I might be interviewing to hire another amazing colleague, speaking to dentists about the opportunities offered by Invisalign or running one of the Mastering your Invisalign Business workshops. The next I could be meeting a potential Network member and finding out all about their practice, or maybe on a conference call with an Align representative to discuss the company's latest innovations.

I'll always find time to take the pulse of my practices, sitting down with my teams every day to keep abreast of everything that's going on and how everyone is feeling. I make a point of carving out some vital space to review the data – you can't make rational decisions if you aren't monitoring data and listening to what it has to say.

Whatever else is going on, I keep myself physically, mentally and emotionally as sharp as possible, so I can deal with whatever gets thrown at me during the day.

What's next for you?

There has never been a better time to expand your dental skills and practice. I hope that the MiSmile blueprint has persuaded you that Invisalign could be the next step for you. It's a venture that you can embark on at your own pace: you can grow slowly, taking on a few more cases every year, or decide from the outset to expand as fast as the take up of your new offer will allow.

The beauty of Invisalign is that it integrates the latest dental technology with the communications technology that people are becoming increasingly comfortable with using, and it creates a genuine community of professionals committed to providing a first-class service with the backing of an established company of international standing. Now that people have come to understand how simple an Invisalign treatment is, and how seamlessly it fits with treatments like bleaching and bonding to provide a 360-degree solution to nearly all cosmetic problems, they are more willing than ever to opt for it.

In joining the MiSmile Network, you will be enhancing your own prospects, along with those of your team and your practice, with the benefit of all the expertise of dedicated professionals who have perfected their approach over many years. Our long-standing relationship with Invisalign ensures that everyone in the Network has access to all the latest developments and innovations, as well as the ongoing training, support and advice to ensure we can offer the best service, no matter how complex the case. I feel proud and privileged to have created such an engaged and enthusiastic group as the MiSmile Network, and I know that all its members find being a part of it hugely rewarding. I would love to welcome you into it.

If you have any feedback – queries, comments, observations – don't hesitate to visit my website or contact me (you can find all my contact details in 'The Author' section). On my website, you'll be able to see for yourself the wide-ranging group of dentists who belong to the MiSmile Network, the testimonials from patients delighted with their new smiles and all the information about the Mastering Your Invisalign Business initiative, which could be your first step towards becoming the owner of a thriving Invisalign practice – and a valued new member of a network of like-minded and supportive professionals.

I look forward to meeting you.

Acknowledgements

My first acknowledgement goes to my wife Rita. She is my rock, my business partner and my best friend. We've had twenty-four years of overcoming challenges, learning, adapting and enjoying the journey of life together. I can't wait to see where our story takes us next.

My next is to my colleague and now lifelong friend Ali Meredith. After a chance introduction back in 2013, I soon realised that Ali just 'got it'. She has been so instrumental in my business growth over the years and has a unique ability to bring my crazy ideas to life. Not afraid to challenge, but always there to support and deliver. Thank you, Ali.

Thirdly to the incredible team at Align Technology. Without our collaboration and partnership, my business model would fall over. From Michael Smith's initial belief in my idea and his commitment to seeing me succeed, to the UK country managers Jamie Morley and Dan Gallagher who I have worked with since 2014. You guys have all supported me on my journey and your critical thinking, inspiration and motivation keep me going.

To Jag Shoker and Justin Leigh, two incredible coaches and mentors who have kept me on track – your focus on my personal development is priceless. Thank you.

Finally, a huge thank you to all the UK dentists who believe in MiSmile and are part of my incredible community. Working with you, watching you grow and prosper is an incredible privilege. Thank you.

The Author

Dr Sandeep Kumar can only be described as a trailblazer in the world of Invisalign. He is one of the UK's leading Invisalign Diamond Apex Providers and has created more than 4,000 beautiful new smiles with Invisalign in his private clinics.

Originally from India, Sandeep came to the UK in 1998. He qualified with the General Dental Council in 2000 and, on the lookout for his next opportunity, bought his first practice in 2003.

When he launched his first private dental clinic in 2007, Sandeep recognised the potential in harnessing

Invisalign's consumer appeal and value to differentiate his practice. He implemented a highly successful lead generation and nurturing process and grew his Invisalign case load from just seven in the first year to 400 cases in 2015. By 2016, he was one of the few UK practitioners to have successfully treated over 2,000 patients with Invisalign.

Sandeep has built his success around the Invisalign clear aligner brand and has inspired and encouraged those he works with to do the same. He now owns three successful dental brands: Smile Dental Birmingham, Smile Stylist and MiSmile, which includes the UK's first Invisalign-only clinic. He also leads the MiSmile Network, made up of a group of more than 100 independent dental clinics across the country, and the Mastering your Invisalign Business programme. He travels round the UK regularly, speaking on the benefits of working with Invisalign and MiSmile or training Network members. As a network, MiSmile has created over 20,000 beautiful new smiles.

He took his vision to a new level in 2021 when he co-founded his new dental brand – Smmmile.

Sandeep may be running a successful commercial business, but through his partnership with the charity Operation Smile, he supports a deeper purpose: the treatment of children born with cleft lips or cleft palates so that they too can have better smiles. It's important to him to be doing something that is making a difference in the world.

Sandeep lives in Birmingham with his wife and family. He loves Formula One and cricket, and he is also a keen cyclist and tennis player. Most evenings he can be found walking in the woods with his dog.

You can connect with Sandeep via:

- www.facebook.com/drsandeepkumardentist
- www.linkedin.com/in/sandeepkumardentist
- www.instagram.com/drsandeepkumar_

Or with his brand via:

- www.facebook.com/MiSmileforDentists
- www.linkedin.com/company/mismile-network
- www.instagram.com/mismilefordentists